LUSITANIA AND BEYOND

The Story of Captain William Turner

Mitch Peeke and Kevin Walsh - Johnson

Illustrated throughout by John Gray

Published by:
Avid Publications
Garth Boulevard
Bebington, Wirral,
Merseyside.
CH63 5LS
Telephone / Fax: (44) 0151 645 2047
e-mail info@AvidPublications.co.uk
website http//www.AvidPublications

Lusitania and Beyond
- the Story of Captain William Turner
by
Mitch Peeke and Kevin Walsh -Johnson
ISBN 1 902964 14 4

Acknowledgements

We would like to gratefully acknowledge the following persons and institutions for their invaluable help and assistance,
Public Records Office, London. National Maritime Museum, Greenwich, London. New York Public Library for the performing arts. New York Public Library. The Museum of the City of New York. Pauline Cass of Liverpool Records Office. University of Liverpool (Cunard archives). Liverpool College records officer, Mr Stott. Hill Dickinson, & Co. Archives Dept. (Cunard's lawyers). Guildhall Library, London. Ogdens Tobacco Co., of Liverpool. Metropolitan Borough of Wirral (Rake Lane Cemetery). Merseyside Maritime Museum, Albert Dock, Liverpool. Barclays Bank. British Titanic Society. Kent County Library Services. Imperial War Museum, London. Royal Artillery Museum, London. Family Records Office, Southport, Merseyside and Islington, London. News International Reference Library, London.

On a more personal level we would also like to thank:
Peter Edward Powell MILC, Mrs Lambert, Mrs Young, Tony and Rose Walsh, Geoff Whitfield, John Adler, Steve Jones, Dick Bottley, Mark Stanford Robbins. For his painstaking proof reading of the draft manuscript, Brian Ticehurst deserves a special mention too.
Very special thanks are due to our wives, Jay and Sonja for their unfailing support in our endeavours, and to John Gray for his splendid illustrations.

A Very Special Acknowledgement

This book could not possibly be regarded as complete without a special acknowledgement to the people of Liverpool. Just how well Captain Turner and the Lusitania are remembered in that fair city was brought home to us by the help we received whilst we were there researching for this book.

It wasn't just people like librarians, records officers or archivists, whose job it was to help, though they all seemed to go that extra mile to find rare information for us, but ordinary people whom we met on the streets, who greeted us and our purpose with a warmth and a friendliness that was quite unexpected.

In fact, a black cab driver that we encountered in Sefton springs to mind. We had gotten ourselves a little lost up there looking for Ormskirk Road. Being black cab drivers ourselves, we naturally turned to him for directions, which he readily gave. On the point of parting, he asked us what we were looking for in the Ormskirk Road, so we told him about Captain Turner. He then asked us if we were sure of the directions he had given us. If not, he offered to lead us to Ormskirk Road without payment. We didn't take him up on this offer as the directions he gave us were spot on, (well, they would be, wouldn't they!) but it was the fact that he was quite prepared to take a chunk out of his working day just to help us, in memory of Captain Turner.

We found that same attitude everywhere we went. Once we had explained our purpose, Police and Security Officers at the Liverpool docks allowed us in, albeit escorted, to take photographs in and around various parts of the docks.

At 50 De Villiers Avenue, Crosby we knocked at the door merely seeking permission to photograph the front exterior of the house. Again, once we had explained ourselves, that "Liverpool warmth" manifested itself. Instead of giving us permission just to photograph the outside, we were invited into Captain Turner's former home, shown around, allowed to take any photographs we wished to take, while today's resident, Mrs. Lambert made a fresh pot of tea for us.

We must have crossed the City of Liverpool half a dozen times on our researching missions, which were a pleasure, but it was on the way home that we realised just how we had been affected.

Driving up to Liverpool, we had been quite excited, talking, planning what to do and where to go on the too few days that we had. Once there, we were of course extremely busy gathering information, checking and cross-checking facts etc. But coming home from Liverpool, we were strangely quiet.

Kevin was driving whilst I was making a few amendments to the draft manuscript we'd taken with us. Suddenly, he asked me how I felt and what impression Liverpool had left on me. I thought about it, then replied, "sad". It was the first time I'd been to Liverpool and I'd found it to be an amazing place full of amazing people, but it struck me that the overall impression Liverpool had made upon me was a sad one.

This was because it appeared to me that Liverpool itself had been drained; milked for all of its commercial worth. I said to Kevin, "It looked to me as if everybody over the last few hundred years had taken whatever they'd wanted from Liverpool, without putting anything back."

Kevin stopped the car at that point. We both sat there for a minute, then Kevin said, "You're right." We decided there and then to do everything we could to (a), get Will Turner's story told, and (b), get it published in his home town if at all possible.

To that end, a final acknowledgement must go to David Roberts of Avid Publications on Merseyside, for listening, and (finally!) agreeing to publish our work. Perhaps between us, we have helped to put a little something back into Liverpool, however small.

v

Introduction

The story of the Lusitania's last voyage has been told many times. The Admiralty investigated it immediately after the disaster of 7th May 1915, with a conclusion to suit their needs, one might add. The wreck has also been the subject of many explorations. As with the Titanic and other ships, media and public interest has been centred on the ships themselves. Few captains of these ships have ever been written about as individuals. With this in mind we decided to research the Captain of the Lusitania, Captain William Thomas Turner.

His is a truly fascinating story. There is so much more to him than just being the captain of a crack liner on an ill-fated voyage.

Most of what is generally told of him has either become blurred with the passage of time, or else shrouded in untruth. He was by no means a simple, uneducated, unbearably stubborn individual. Nor was he a treacherous knave in the pay of the Germans.

He was an outstanding seaman who had learned his trade and mastered it, the hard way - by experience. He grew up in a time of unchanging moral values for he was primarily a Victorian man. His outlook on life and the world was from the vantage point at the zenith of the British Empire and was tempered with his own set of personal standards, which were high. His was an age of ever advancing technology and a deep-rooted pride in his country's achievements. He was a patriot, though not of the jingoistic type sometimes associated with his era.

The Edwardian era, short though it was, was a natural sequel to the Victorian age and for people like Will Turner, a logical progression. But the events of August 1914 and afterwards, turned his world and the worlds of many like him, upside down; shattering all his beliefs about life, people and the way of the world. After 1914, that world would never be the same again.

Will Turner was undoubtedly a mild eccentric. He was also a strict disciplinarian. Yet his crews loved him for it, as did his passengers. Enigmatic then, but the best way to gain an insight into this remarkable man is to read his story. We hope that through the pages of this book, you can come to know the man who was Captain William Thomas Turner.

CONTENTS

Dedicated to the memory of:

James William Barry,

Ben Bennett

and Captain William Thomas Turner.

Also dedicated with much love to:

Katie, Maddie, Lucy and Lisa.

Beginnings...

Ⅰn the mid nineteenth Century, the port of Liverpool was a bustling hive of activity. The docks ran for nearly seven miles along the River Mersey and at any given time, over one hundred sailing ships of every description from the smallest schooner to the biggest barque, could be counted in the docks loading or unloading.

All around the cobbled wharves, horses pulled carts laden with goods, which were either bound for, or had just arrived from, far off places. Every corner of the wharves had stacks of kegs and barrels. Coils of ropes lay at the side of every gangway and the whole area resounded to the calls and shouts of dockers, working in gangs to manhandle cargoes between the ships and the many high walled warehouses that surrounded the basins. The sound of the various ship's bells provided an almost musical accompaniment.

One could smell the docks from a considerable distance. The river itself, rope, tar, paint, horses and grease, all mingled with fish, meat, exotic spices, flour, cotton, tobacco and timber to imbue the whole area with a distinctive and somewhat heady aroma all of its own. Towering above all this, sometimes to heights of nearly 200 feet, was the forest of masts and yards, upon which the Liverpool docks were dependent.

The smell of coal smoke from the little steam tugs made a sort of novelty value contribution to the aroma of the docks. Steam was slowly making inroads but sail, the traditional method of propulsion, still very much held the upper hand. The big liners had not yet arrived to steal the thunder. In time, the steel mammoths would monopolise the world's shipping, but that was still 40 years away.

In port, a sailing ship's crew was never idle. The ship's mates saw to that. Be it overhauling the ship's rigging, scraping and painting the hull or taking on fresh supplies, there was always something to do under the mate's watchful eye.

Liverpool Docks circa 1880

The Captain of a sailing ship was distinguishable by the fact that his appearance was somewhat tidier than that of the ordinary crewmember, for these were the days before gold braided uniforms. God forbid that ship owners like Beazley, Wilson, Gracie, Brocklebank or James Baines, the celebrated but irascible owner of the Black Ball Line, should be made to look less important in public than one of their captains. The wearing of tidy clothes and a bowler hat when ashore on ship's business was usually sufficient to mark the wearer as a ship's Captain. Fine suits were most definitely the preserve of the ship owners.

In those days an owner would sometimes accompany his ship on a voyage. In such circumstances the owner was known as the ship's Master and the Captain was in command of the crew. The Captain's chief responsibility was the navigation of the ship. Crew discipline was usually handled by the first mate, with the Captain being the final arbiter. The Master issued his instructions to the Captain whose job it was to carry them out in a seaman like manner, but as expeditiously as possible.

Later as the fleets of the merchant ship owners grew, they no longer took the voyages themselves. Captains now became "Master under God" and took full responsibility for the ship, crew and cargo. A good Captain was strict but fair and if necessary drove his ship and crew with the mailed fist of a Roman Centurion. A fast passage was the aim of every Captain, but a first rate Captain knew the limits to which safety as well as the crew could be pushed. It was no good "Cracking on" to make the fastest passage if it ended in disaster with ship and cargo lost, as in the case of the celebrated Captain Jock Sutherland's last voyage, which wrecked the *Holt Hill*. He did this during a violent tropical storm, running her straight into an island in the Indian Ocean, carrying all sail merely because there had been another ship in sight and Sutherland was determined that the *Holt Hill* would not be overtaken.

Nor was there any glory in finishing first but with only half of the crew prepared to make the return leg of the journey. A good Captain was one who got the best out of his ship and crew by earning

3

Working life of a sailor- late 19th century

their respect and in return would get that crew to follow him to the very ends of the earth out of sheer loyalty as opposed to the kind of fear which Captains like "Bully Forbes" were known to instill. His technique consisted of padlocking the braces then standing at the break of the poop with the keys to the padlocks in one hand and a loaded pistol in the other, the wind and seas raging all around him, and threatening to shoot the first man to go aloft without his permission to shorten sail. "This ship will reach Hell or Melbourne in 60 days, and I don't care which it is!" he would bellow at his crew. His record shows that although he came as close to making a 60 day passage to Melbourne as was humanly possible, it was his own personal Hell that Captain James Nichol Forbes reached first.

One example of a man who would later become one of the better types, a good type of Captain, was Charles Turner of Clarence Street, Liverpool. In 1856 at the age of 29, he was already married with one daughter, Annie Maria who was two. On October 23rd of that year his wife Charlotte bore him a son whom they called William Thomas Turner.

Charles Turner was already making a name for himself as a fine first mate since obtaining his Master's certificate, No. C8754, only three years previously.

At the time of William's birth, Clarence Street was a small street of neat terraced houses in the Everton district of Liverpool. Though set well back from the waterfront, they overlooked the area of the Albert Dock and it would have been possible for William to watch the arrival and departure of the ships using the port. Doubtlessly, he would have maintained a special watch for his father's ship whenever it was due.

Living so near to the busy, thriving docks, William soon developed a natural fascination for the sea and the ships that sailed the world's Oceans. He began to yearn for the sailor's life.

In 1864, when William was eight years of age, Charles took him aboard his ship. Young William enjoyed every minute of it. Standing on the main deck looking skyward at the towering masts and

5

the mass of attendant rigging, filled him with wonderment and the seeds of his future were sown. Despite this, Charles actually tried to dissuade his son from following in his footsteps. He knew only too well the rigours and sacrifices of a life at sea and he wanted better for his son. Charles wanted his son to pursue a career in the Church as a Minister. His son however, mature beyond his tender years due to being the man of the house during his father's long absences, was adamant and in no doubt about where his future lay and that was at sea. Even at that age, he knew himself well enough after the long hours spent at the dockside talking to the sailors and watching the ships whilst waiting for his father's ship to return, to know that he did not want "the Clerical life of a Devil-dodger," as he later put it, and the more his father tried to steer him away from the sea, the more his seagoing resolve hardened. Will Turner's early years in Clarence Street overlooking the vast port, would have been an inspiration to any young boy wishing to embark on a life at sea.

Whether it was the romance of sail or the thought of all those far off exotic places that set Will's heart on a sea career, nobody now knows. Possibly it was both, but one thing was certain, Will had heard the call of the sea and he was determined to respond to it.

So it was that in 1869, at the age of 13, young William was fast approaching manhood. In those days, the school leaving age (assuming the child's parents were sufficiently placed to be able to send their child to school) was 14. Having maintained his resolve to go to sea, and with Charles now having abandoned his attempts to convince his son otherwise, Will Turner finally managed to persuade his parents to allow him to discontinue his studies, although he was a promising student, leave school and embark upon a life at sea. Will was resolute that one day he was going to be a ship's Captain, just like his father.

Learning the ropes…

Will found himself a berth on a ship called the *Grasmere*, a small barque of 432 tons built in 1847. Filled with a boy's enthusiasm and driven by his earlier experiences, Will sailed on his first real voyage. The steam tug towed the *Grasmere* out of the docks into the Mersey estuary and said farewell to them at Liverpool Bay. The Captain gave a stream of orders and the ship's hands went aloft to loose the sails. As the wind filled her sails the *Grasmere* began to move through the water. Picking up speed the braces were manned and the crew began to sing as they hauled on the ropes. The sounds of the billowing canvas sails and the ship cutting through the water were music to Will's ears. This was truly wondrous!

However, young Will soon came to have a greater understanding of the power of the sea. A gale sprang up quite quickly soon after their departure from Liverpool. The stiff breeze that gave the ship her sail, gave way to a violent gale. Rain, gale force winds and deck-high waves battered the ship relentlessly. The once secure cargo was now loose and tossed about the ship causing mayhem, then washed overboard. The calm sea that welcomed Will on his first voyage was now showing him all her fury. The Captain and crew put up a brave fight but eventually the *Grasmere* was driven onto a submerged reef off the Northern Irish coast at County Antrim, near Belfast. *Grasmere* foundered and Will found himself having to swim for his life through rock-strewn waters in the teeth of the gale. Fortunately for him, Will could swim like a dolphin. Tired and battered he pulled himself ashore having learned a salutary lesson in what the sea could do.

Will Turner's sea career hadn't exactly got off to an auspicious start. However, despite the setback of being shipwrecked on his first voyage whilst still in home waters, he was undaunted. The formalities of the shipwreck, such as the mandatory crew depositions to the Board of Trade over, Will's father took a hand in finding him another ship to

Learning the ropes aboard the White Star

Some examples of sailing ship knots

sail in. It did not take him long to find his son a place in the crew of his old ship, the *White Star*

The *White Star* was a renowned clipper of 2,217 tons owned by the Merchant's Trading Company Limited of Liverpool, for whom Charles worked. Charles managed to secure Will a berth as cabin boy under the command of his friend, Captain Jones. *White Star* was bound from Liverpool to Aden round the Cape of Good Hope and on to the Guanape islands off the coast of Ecuador. The voyage would prove to be a good start to Will's sea education. The expression "to be shown the ropes" is still widely used today and it is a sailing ship expression. A fast Clipper like the *White Star* had in excess of 450 different ropes all controlling different functions. A sailor had to know what each one of those ropes did by instinct. There were Buntlines, Clewlines, Sheets, Braces, Downhauls, Lifts, Halliards, Shrouds; to name but a few. As well as knowing the ropes and functions Will had to learn all the different ways of tying them; Bowline on the bight, Figure of eight, Reef knot, Sheep shank, Fisherman's bend, Sheet Bend; these were functional knots and woe betide anyone who used the wrong knot for any given purpose. As well as the functional knots there was a whole host of decorative knots which Will took a particular pleasure in learning.

But there was a lighter side to the subjects to be learned and one of them was the making of "Dandyfunk". The food on a nineteenth century sailing ship had not improved much at all since the eighteenth century. The fresh provisions with which a ship started a voyage soon ran out. "Salt junk" and improvisation then became a sailors' diet. Salt junk was meat, which had been preserved in pure salt and was usually rock hard chunks of beef if you were lucky. More usually it was horsemeat. Dandyfunk is a traditional delicacy of deep water sailing ship crews. It is primarily a way of supposedly making the iron hard ship's biscuits more palatable.

To make Dandyfunk, a boy had first to befriend the ship's cook. This was usually accomplished by way of favours like helping out in the galley. Next the boy must make a small canvas bag. Into the canvas

10

bag are put a quantity of the ship's biscuits from which the resident weevils have been evicted, and then the bag is taken on deck and pounded with a belaying pin until the biscuits are reduced to a uniform mass of crumbs. To the crumbs is added a sufficient quantity of grease (the stuff used to lubricate the yards and masts usually) to make something, that resembled dough. This dough was then given to the cook who would add "something nice" to give it flavour, cinnamon or ginger was the common and magical ingredient. The dough was then spread into a flat tin tray and baked, whilst the crew eagerly awaited the outcome.

With the Barometer reading "set fair" and the North East Trade Wind pushing the *White Star* Southwestwards at a respectable pace under clear blue skies, the crew did not have much to do in the way of working the ship. This was the time for more routine maintenance to be carried out. Overhauling the rigging was an ongoing process that Will would actively participate in. He was taught how to splice ropes, grease the masts and yards, repair blocks and make gaskets. Once proficient at these basic aspects of seamanship, he was taught how to "Box the Compass" and steer the ship. He also learned the value of a good shanty when the work was hard and laborious, as it often was.

The early stage of the voyage was also an ideal time to build up the boy's physical strength for the trials that lay ahead. Will would develop muscles he never knew he had working aloft. He would certainly need them later!

As *White Star* ventured into the tropics, Will came to know why the rest of the crew began to grumble about entering the "Horse Latitudes". This region may be more familiar to you by the name of "The Doldrums". It is a region either side of the Equator where the winds suddenly die away, leaving a sailing ship becalmed. Sailors always referred to it as the Horse Latitudes because they knew that the Captain would have them working like horses, changing the ship's tack to catch every faint breath of wind, from whichever direction it came, in a supreme effort to make some sort of headway, however slight.

11

It frequently took days to escape the doldrums and the morale of the crew would often hit a low point during this part of the voyage. However, the ceremony of "crossing the line" usually helped to relieve any tensions in the crew. This is still a ritualistic initiation ceremony for any member of a ship's crew who has never crossed the Equator before. The crew elect a King Neptune and then set up his court. The unfortunate "first-timers" are brought before the King after having first undergone some ghastly preparation procedures, mostly of an unpleasant nature, which usually finish with the victim being daubed with bright green paint to represent his inexperience. Once King Neptune has given his "blessing" to the unfortunate individual, he is formally accepted into the crew.

Once across the Equator and out of the doldrums, there was work a-plenty. The crew would have to take every sail down, one at a time, and change the fair weather canvas for the storm canvas. Heavy work indeed, and a sailor was as likely to suffer a sore throat from singing shanties as well as calloused and blistered hands from hauling on the ropes.

Once the canvas had all been changed there was another job of work to be done that was dreaded by every crew on every sailing ship that ever sailed the world's Oceans. "Holystoning" the deck was backbreaking work of the very worst kind. The crew always knew the task was looming when the ship's Carpenter was suddenly seen making a heavy wooden frame with a rope at each corner. The frame was laid on the deck and a quantity of coarse sand poured into it. With a man on the rope at each corner, the frame was slowly hauled backwards and forwards, for a distance of about three feet at a time, sanding the deck in the process. With the ship entering the Southern latitudes, where sudden tropical storms were frequent, they could not afford to have the deck even the slightest degree slippery. The whole of the Main deck would have to be sanded in this manner with every member of the crew taking his turn at the frame. The crew knew that their lives could easily depend upon how well this work was carried out, but it was a loathsome task all the same.

The voyage progressed, though not perhaps as quickly as Captain Jones may have wished. *White Star* called at Aden, then crossed the Indian Ocean, passed the great continent of Australia, and finally traversed the Pacific Ocean to arrive at the Guanape Islands, there to drop her anchor. By this time, he had become an accepted member of the crew, but the Guanape Islands held a surprise for Will Turner.

Also at anchor there, was the newest ship of the Merchant's Trading Company, which he knew by sight, she was the 1,462-ton *Queen of Nations*. Will also knew that this was her Captain's first command and in a short space of time his transfer to the *Queen of Nations* was agreed and completed. Will's next voyage was from the Guanape Islands to Callao then homeward bound for Liverpool under the command of Captain Charles Turner.

The return voyage was by the way of the notorious Cape Horn, home to permanent gales and mountainous seas. The huge waves found there are known as "Greybeards" and the region is known to all sailors as "The Roaring Forties." Rounding the Horn in a sailing ship has never been easy. It is a supreme test of skills and seamanship and many a ship and crew has come to grief in the region. Any ship that found herself broached to the waves (lying across them) was lost. Hurricane force winds and waves 45 feet in height are the normal weather and sea conditions off the Horn. To successfully round the Horn was to know elation that was complete, tempered with the sheer relief at survival of the worst weather possible. To fail was death and this was Will's first time around the Horn.

Will had often listened to his father's tales of rounding the Horn. He'd sat enthralled as Charles told him of the shrieking winds, the huge waves, the driving rain, of sails and yards and sometimes even masts being carried away. Of green seas coming aboard and swamping the decks. Of the crewmen washed overboard never to be seen again, for there was no possible way of rescuing them. Of the ship's lifeboats being smashed to pieces by the relentless violence of the Cape Horn weather.

Storm brewing off the Horn – Queen of Nations

Going aloft in bad weather off the Horn - Queen of Nations

Into a trough off the Horn – Queen of Nations

Off Cape Horn. seas swamp the deck – Queen of Nations

But to sit at home snug and warm listening to his father recount these events was one thing, to experience it at first hand as Will was about to do, was quite another.

The approaching gale struck quite suddenly and without any warning as the Cape Horn gale usually does. "All hands aloft and shorten sail!" shouted Captain Turner. No exceptions were made, young Will may have been a boy not quite 14 years of age and the Captain's son, but he'd already served enough of his apprenticeship to know that on a sailing ship you did a mans work regardless of age or size. All hands meant all hands.

As the winds increased in velocity and the seas mounted ever higher, lashing rain adding to the tumult. "One hand for yourself and the other hand for the ship", the old seaman's maxim, took on its full meaning, as there were no safety devices whatsoever. The only aids a sailor had aloft were the footrope and his wits.

The sails had to be taken in quickly before the wind carried them away, or worse, lest the ship become dismasted and helpless. It soon became apparent to the more seasoned members of the crew that this was a gale even fiercer than was usual in these latitudes. As they fought with the wildly flapping canvas and the ship heaving and rolling beneath them, it happened. The sails could not be gathered in quickly enough and with a series of loud bangs and cracks which were barely audible above the noise of the storm, most of her canvas and some of the yards were carried away leaving a mass of broken ropes, blocks and timbers wildly thrashing about aloft. For the crew, it was a pitched battle all the way. Their ship was now carrying only a bare minimum of sail, but the *Queen of Nations* finally managed to round the Horn and escape the Roaring Forties, but what a sight she was.

Captain Turner realised his ship would never make it home in her derelict condition. She had taken a real battering and was also shipping water; not fast, but steadily enough and it would only get worse. Faced with the situation he decided to jettison the cargo, some 300 tons in weight, to save the ship and *Queen of Nations* limped to the Falkland Islands and put in for repairs.

The repairs delayed the voyage for over three months, but for Will the time was not spent idly. He still had much to learn about shipboard life. By the time *Queen of Nations* left the Falklands and was homeward bound, Will had laid the foundations of his sea career. His confidence and his skills were steadily growing, as he was himself. When the *Queen of Nations* finally docked in Liverpool, Will had spent a year under the command of his father. It was time for a change, for the both of them. Charles joined the Cunard line, his son changed ships.

Will's next ship was a full rigger, the *War Spirit* of 1,190 tons, which again sailed from Liverpool. Will signed on as an able seaman for another around the world voyage. This trip, like the last was to prove memorable for him as it included an outbreak of yellow fever amongst the *War Spirit*'s crew. Unlike a number of the ship's crew who succumbed to yellow fever Will was lucky. Yellow fever was found in South American Countries. The disease starts by causing sudden high temperatures, black vomit and finally a lowering of the pulse rate until death. This virulent disease remained unchecked, even delaying the building of the Panama Canal due to the afflicted labour force, until Walter Reed, an American army surgeon and bacteriologist, finally connected the Stegomyia Mosquito with the virus in 1901. Only then could measures be taken to deal with the disease.

The return trip out of St. John, New Brunswick, saw the *War Spirit*'s deck cargo washed overboard in heavy seas. The vessel was also shipping water. Wallowing badly and riding very low in the water, she drifted helplessly for four days until a passing steamer sighted them and towed them into a Spanish port.

Upon his return to England Will changed his home port to London and served on the *Duncraig*, a small barque of 740 tons and then the *Royal Alfred*, an iron hulled barque of 1,239 tons under Captain Fisher. During his "off watch" hours he diligently studied the principles and practices of navigation, striving all the time to achieve his dream, his Master's ticket. He also taught himself to play the fiddle.

19

By the time he'd passed for third mate on the *Royal Alfred* he was already studying for his second mate's certificate, which he wasn't long in attaining. His keenness to get on always showed itself, as did his often dry sense of humour. "I was the fastest man aloft in a sailing ship," he would often tell people later, "except for a Greek I once met. He must have had a monkey as an ancestor and not so very remote either!"

One of Will's favourite stories concerns an incident which befell him whilst he was second mate under Captain Couth on a very famous clipper called the *Thunderbolt*, of 1,193 tons and bound for Calcutta. It was the monsoon season and Will was off watch on the bowsprit, fishing. Suddenly he was swept overboard by a "comber." As the ship passed him, the first mate threw him a lifebuoy from the quarterdeck and shouted, "Man overboard!" The crew were quick to react, but Will still had to wait whilst they wore the ship around, which took over an hour and a quarter to accomplish.

Whilst the crew of the *Thunderbolt* moved mountains to turn the ship round, Will had perceived a greater problem for himself; SHARKS! Clinging to his lifebuoy, he was becoming the main attraction for them. There began an earnest battle that lasted for just under an hour. Will fought the sharks off with kicks, shouts and even punches, whilst seeing his plight the *Thunderbolt's* crew were frantically coming to his rescue.

Rescue him they did, though not before one persistent shark was finally dissuaded by a sharp upper cut from Will who was by now approaching exhaustion and would soon have lost the uneven struggle.

As he finally clambered up the rope ladder which the crew had put over the side for him, he heard the voice of Captain Couth call out in his familiar martinet's tone," Is that you Mister Turner?!" The Captain of course knew full well who it was. " It is sir," Will replied, with barely enough breath to say so. "Well you can come aboard and go to your bunk for three days." And as Will finally made it over the rail onto the deck dripping wet and with barely sufficient strength left to stand, in an unusually kindly manner Captain Couth added, "By the way Mister Turner, don't forget to empty your watch before you turn in, or the water will rust the works."

2nd Mate W.T. Turner overboard from Thunderbolt

After two further voyages aboard the *Thunderbolt*, Will Turner realised that as much as he loved sailing vessels, the mariner's future lay in steamships. It was not an easy decision for him to make but he had to accept it. Once more he returned to his beloved Liverpool and joined the Inman line as a junior officer. He served briefly as Fourth Officer on the liner *City of Chester*, making only two voyages and also on the Leyland liner *Egyptian*. During all this time he was still studying navigation, never once slackening the pace of his learning.

The year was now 1878. Fourth Officer William Thomas Turner had just turned 22 years of age and although he did not yet know it, his next decision was to shape the rest of his seagoing career. In October 1878 Will Turner joined the Cunard Line.

Cunard Line...

The Cunard steamship company was founded in 1840, by Samuel Cunard with the express intention of tendering for the lucrative transatlantic mail contracts. These were attractive by virtue of the subsidies granted by the Admiralty, who were responsible for the mails. However, it wasn't all in favour of the steamship owner as the Admiralty benefited considerably too. Some of the clauses included stiff penalties for missed sailings and delays but were more than worth it and what is more, the amounts paid to shipping companies were reviewable.

From the Admiralty's point of view, those new steamship lines represented a training ground for naval personnel. Two other conditions imposed were the presence on board these steamers of an officer of the Royal Navy to "safeguard" the mails and a stipulation that the ships themselves be capable of mounting heavy guns, should a national emergency arise. Thus on May 4th 1839, much to the dismay of rival tenders who pointed out that Samuel Cunard did not yet own any ships, the contracts were signed and thus was born the special relationship between the Cunard company and the British government by way of their agent, the British Admiralty.

On July 4th 1840 at 14.00 hours on a wet and windy day, Cunard's first ship, the 1,156 ton *Britannia*, left Liverpool under the command of Captain Henry Woodruff RN on her maiden voyage to Halifax, Nova Scotia.

Over the course of the next few years as Cunard prospered, additional negotiations secured arrangements whereby in the event of war Cunard would have to supply ships for government services like troop transport. In return, the ever-obliging Admiralty increased Cunard's subsidy and no longer required the presence of a Naval officer aboard Cunard steamers.

By the time the Crimean war broke out in 1854, Cunard's fleet of transatlantic steamers had grown from just the *Britannia* of 1840, to sixteen ships. The Admiralty's annual subsidy had grown from £55,000 in 1840 to more than £158,000 in 1854. During the Crimean war the strength of the special relationship was put to the test and Cunard supplied eleven of their sixteen ships for government service.

In 1856 the Crimean war ended and Cunard went back to the North Atlantic service. This was interrupted again during the American civil war of 1863, but Cunard weathered this storm by trading in war supplies. The American civil war came to an end in 1865, as did Samuel Cunard's life, on the 28th April. At the time of his death he was a Baronet and died as Sir Samuel Cunard.

By 1870, just as Will was putting to sea aboard *White Star*, Cunard was the dominant name on the North Atlantic, but competition from the White Star Line was already making itself felt. When Will joined Cunard in 1878, the rivalry between Cunard and White Star was just beginning. His first Cunard appointment was as Third Officer on the steamer *Cherbourg*.

Cherbourg was quite a small steamer at only 1,614 tons. She was built in 1875 for Cunard's Mediterranean service and with a maximum speed of 10 knots, she was not exactly a flyer. Cargo carrying was her prime function, but to help with costs she had accommodation for four passengers travelling first class. Insignificant she may have seemed, but as often happened on a voyage involving Will Turner, this little ship was about to bring him to the attention of others in spectacular fashion.

The morning of *Cherbourg's* departure from Liverpool was shrouded in dense fog. Steaming slowly out of the Huskisson dock, the *Cherbourg* collided with a barque, the *Alice Davies*. The *Cherbourg* was immediately halted, but the *Alice Davies* was sinking rapidly. Will Turner and a rescue party from the *Cherbourg* got there in time to save most of those aboard the stricken vessel, though the pilot and four of *Alice Davies'* crewmen were drowned. Will personally saved one man and a boy who had climbed up the rigging of the sinking vessel. Neither vessel was blamed for the incident as *Cherbourg's* speed was prudently low, and both vessels had been following the due procedure for the prevailing weather conditions. But the incident was favourably noted on Will Turner's record.

Meanwhile the White Star line's *Oceanic, Republic, Baltic* and *Atlantic* had more than made their presence on the North Atlantic felt, they had dominated it. These four ships outshone the entire Cunard fleet in every respect. Everyone's eyes were on the transatlantic route, for emigration from Europe to "The New World" of North America was at an all time high. In 1881, Cunard were finally able to rise to the White Star Line's challenge with the commissioning of their new ship, *Servia.* Steel hulled and capable of seventeen knots, she was the first of the express liners to rely solely on passenger revenue by a means of a fast passage. In addition, she was also the first liner to have electric lighting on board. It was a bold step for Cunard, but it was the way ahead.

For Will though, the prestige of the North Atlantic run was still some way off. He was still holding the rank of Third Officer on the not quite so important Mediterranean service. He was striving all the while for his Master's ticket and was moved to a slightly larger ship called *Aleppo.*

One frigid February morning in 1883, Will was walking by the Alexandra dock in Liverpool on his way to join his ship. Suddenly there was a commotion on the dockside. He hurried to see what it was all about though he really did not have time to linger.

A small crowd was gathering at the dockside and as he got closer he could hear gasps from the crowd, some of who were pointing to the water. Will pushed his way to the front and quickly saw the cause of the scene. A 14 year old boy had fallen into the icy water and it was immediately obvious to him that the boy couldn't swim.

, Pausing only to take off his shoes, cap and greatcoat, Will jumped into the freezing water and swam to the boy's aid. The sheer coldness of the water was like a thousand knives being driven into his body, but his only thought was of rescue. Upon reaching him, he found that the lad had almost stopped struggling to survive. Will quickly took him in the lifesaver's tow and some men in the crowd helped to pull them both out of the water once they had regained the dockside.

For this outstanding example of selfless courage, Will Turner was awarded the silver medal for saving life at sea, by the Liverpool Shipwreck and Humane Society. Happily the boy survived his ordeal.

With his ambition of captaining a ship still driving him on, Will made a discovery which forced him to change the direction of his career temporarily. Cunard had a strict policy regarding the captains of their ships. They would not promote an officer to Master, no matter how outstanding his record was, until he had commanded a square rigged sailing ship. As the Cunard steamship company possessed no such vessel, he would have to leave Cunard in order to gain the necessary certificate. In April of 1883, Will Turner duly left Cunard and returned to the world of billowing canvas that he knew and loved so well. For the next three years, he voyaged across the world's Oceans as second mate, gaining the necessary theoretical knowledge as well as the practical experience needed to sit his Master's exam.

Back to the wind…

The year 1886 was a landmark year in his life. In his home port of Liverpool, Will Turner successfully sat and passed his Board of Trade ship's Master exam. He was awarded certificate No. 02168 and certified as "Square Rig Master" for foreign-going ships. Two years later, having now served now as first mate in sail, first under Captain Gardiner on the 1,459-ton full rigger, *Royal George* and lastly under Captain Wood on a similar, though newer ship, the *Prince Frederick*, he returned to Cunard armed with his Master's ticket, though as yet he still had not commanded a sailing ship. But that was about to change.

01268

By The Lords of the Committee of Privy
Council for Trade

Certificate of Competency
MASTER
OF A SQUARE RIG SHIP.

To ___ William Thomas Turner ___

Whereas it has been reported to us that you have been found duly qualified to fulfil the duties of Master of a Square rig Ship in the Merchant Service, we do hereby, in pursuance of the Merchant Shipping Act 1872, grant you this Certificate of Competency.

By Order of the Board of Trade,
this ___ 30th ___ day of ___ September ___ 18 86.

Countersigned, Henry L Mailer
Registrar General

Walter J. Howle { One of the Assst. Secretaries to the Board of Trade

Registered at the Office of the Registrar General of Shipping and Seamen.

Artists impression of William Turner's Masters Certificate – based upon a contemporary certificate

Having outlined his intentions to Cunard he was immediately promoted to Second Officer on March 1st 1888. The next day, he joined the Cunard steamship *Etruria* as Second Officer for one voyage to the United States. Just over one year later on March 27th, 1889, Will Turner sailed out of New York harbour bound for Australia, as Captain of a three masted barque called " *Star of the East.*" To mark the occasion, he resurrected an old sailing ship custom. Just before *Star of the East* sailed, Will purchased a brand new bowler hat. It was a tradition he maintained until his retirement and it would later earn him the nickname of "Bowler Bill". Very few people understood it, but nobody dared call him by it to his face.

As a newly qualified Captain, Will had a lot to live up to, but his years of experience in all aspects of deep water sailing ships were to stand him in very good stead. The life of every sailor on a sailing ship was a hard life, he knew that from his own experiences. He knew too that if a good crew had a bad Captain or a Captain who was overly harsh and mean with them, it would be a recipe for disaster. But he also knew that if the Captain was too easy going, or soft, then any crew would be only too willing to take advantage of such a Captain and he would never get the best out of the crew or ship. From the outset therefore, he ran a tight ship, strict but fair. His role model was undoubtedly his father, who by now was a "Master Mariner". Will's character developed into a unique blend of his father and Captain Couth, under whom he'd served on the *Thunderbolt*, backed by his own skill and judgement based upon personal experience. It was a truly remarkable blend and produced a quite extraordinary man.

The Star of the East's round voyage to Australia was almost a re-run of his first real voyage on the *White Star*, except of course that he was now in command of the ship. Odd really, but it seemed that this was the only profession whereby one started at the top (of the mast) and gradually worked one's way down! Still, standing on the quarterdeck, looking up at the billowing sails of a tall ship that was ploughing her way over the gentle swell of the deep Ocean, and this time knowing that he was in command as Master under God, must have been an exhilarating experience for Will Turner. Perhaps only the classic sailor's poem, *SEA-FEVER*, by John Masefield, could best describe the reflective nature of a shipboard moment such as this.

I must go down to the seas again, to the lonely sea and the sky.
And all I ask is a tall ship and a star to steer her by.
And the wheel's kick and the wind's song and the white sail's shaking.
And a grey mist on the sea's face and a grey dawn breaking.

I must go down to the seas again, for the call of the running tide
Is a wild call and a clear call that may not be denied;
And all I ask is a windy day with the white clouds flying,
And the flung spray and the blown spume, and the sea-gulls crying.

I must go down to the seas again, to the vagrant gypsy life,
To the gull's way and the whale's way, where the wind's like a whetted knife;
And all I ask is a merry yarn from a laughing fellow-rover,
And a quiet sleep and a sweet dream, when the long trick's over.

The round voyage proved to be a good one. Ship and crew had given their all and the ship's owner, Sir W. Cameron, was more than happy to write a glowing letter of testimony to the attributes of Captain William Thomas Turner.

In August of 1890, Will Turner left the world of sail behind him and rejoined Cunard. The following month he was duly promoted to the rank of First Officer and appointed to the steamship *Cephalonia* on the North Atlantic run.

28

Aboard 'Star of the East'. Captain Turner using his sextant.

Long Haul...

During Will's five-year absence, Cunard had not been idle. In 1885, in response to the White Star Line's ascendancy, Cunard had challenged with two new ships, *Etruria* and *Umbria*, which completely outclassed their rivals. The White Star Line responded in 1888 with two magnificent ships, *Majestic* and *Teutonic*. Cunard then ordered two more ships, which were to be the largest, finest and fastest ships in the world; *Campania* and *Lucania*. These ships were another bold step forward for Cunard as they were the first vessels to be built without auxiliary sails.

Will served as *Cephalonia's* First Officer until the end of January 1892. On February 18th 1892 he was promoted to Chief Officer and reappointed in that capacity to his old ship *Aleppo* back on the Mediterranean service. He made 19 round voyages of this kind and was then appointed Chief Officer of the *Catalonia* on August 26th, 1895, on the Liverpool to New York run.

It was also somewhere about this time that Will got married and was living at 31 Springfield Road, Sale, Manchester. Unfortunately, virtually nothing is known of this marriage, as despite exhaustive enquiries at the Family Records Offices both in Southport, Merseyside and London, records of it do not appear. We were told that this is by no means an uncommon occurrence as a large number of such records were lost to the actions of the Luftwaffe during the last war. One assumes that the marriage started happily enough, but for some reason or other, his relationship with his wife deteriorated rapidly after the birth of their second son, Percy. The exact reasons for this are not known, as in those days especially, one did not speak of such things openly.

Meanwhile, Cunard were now the undisputed holders of the Blue Riband of the North Atlantic, thanks to *Campania* and *Lucania*

Umbria / Etruria

who constantly vied with each other. Between them they had pushed the speed up to 21.75 knots and reduced the crossing time of the Atlantic to five days and eight hours. Cunard would never formally recognise the Blue Riband, as their prime concern was passenger safety and not "Ocean racing" as a company spokesman once publicly stated.

On March 6th, 1896 Will was appointed to the *Bothnia* as Chief Officer on the Liverpool to Boston service. He served briefly one year later on *Bothnia's* sister ship, *Gallia* and was then reappointed to *Catalonia* in June of 1897. In September of 1897, on his last voyage as Chief Officer of the *Catalonia*, they sighted a French schooner, the *Vagne*, dismasted and sinking in heavy seas off the Grand Banks of Newfoundland. Despite the weather, a volunteer rescue party from the *Catalonia*, led by Will Turner, succeeded in rescuing the entire crew of the *Vagne* just before she sank, using *Catalonia's* emergency boat as a ferry. One of the *Catalonia's* leading stokers, who was a member of the rescue party, wrote a short poem about the rescue, one verse of which was dedicated to his Chief Officer, William Thomas Turner. The following extract was reproduced later in a Liverpool newspaper:-

31

"The Captain gave his orders to the mate
to man the boat in spite of fate
and then brave Turner looked around
and to his men said, "Come on"
Brave Turner is a man of British pluck:
he's a credit to old England, and Will
always have good luck"

Not exactly Pulitzer prize material, but genuine and heartfelt all the same. 1897 was also notable for Will Turner for another reason. It was the year in which he passed for Extra Master. This was an additional qualification to his Master's certificate and may be best described as "advanced navigation". It also meant that as far as qualifications went William Thomas Turner was now at the top of the tree. On a closing note for Queen Victoria's diamond jubilee year of 1897, he was summoned to Liverpool town hall on December 17th for the presentation, by the Lord Mayor, of a medal from the Mercantile Marine Service Association, (of which Will was a committee member), for his part in the rescue of the crew of the *Vagne*. Also present were the *Catalonia's* Captain and senior officers plus the Captain and officers of the Cunard liner *Etruria*, who had mounted a rescue in similar circumstances, of the crew of the steamer *Millfield*.

As 1897 gave way to 1898, Will completed three round trips to America. One on the *Sylvania* and two on the *Aurania*. He was then appointed Chief Officer on the 8,128 ton *Umbria*. After 12 round transatlantic crossings the *Umbria* was called up for government service.

On December 29th 1899, *Umbria* sailed to South Africa. The Boer war had broken out and *Umbria* was required as a troop carrier. She rendered signal service in this capacity and in July of 1900 she was returned to her former transatlantic role. Will had served on her throughout but upon her return from South Africa he would make only three more round transatlantic crossings with her. On October 4th 1900 Will stepped aboard the former Blue Riband holder, *Lucania*, as her Chief Officer. She sailed on the noontide of that day.

By 1900, *Campania* and *Lucania* were no longer the fastest ships on the North Atlantic. That title now belonged to the Germans. The *Kaiser Wilhelm Der Grosse*, of the Norddeutscher Lloyd line, had been the first to wrest the Blue Riband from Cunard's grasp. But *Campania* and *Lucania* were still the two principal Cunard ships and *Lucania* was a world apart from the Cunarders that Will was used to.

At 12,952 tons, *Lucania* was half as big again as *Umbria*. She was also 100 feet longer than *Umbria*, nearly three knots faster and carried 650 more passengers. More importantly for Will though, *Lucania* carried a crew of 400. This meant that Will was directly responsible to the Captain for himself and 398 others. Plus there were the usual shipboard duties of a Chief Officer to attend to and of course, one mustn't forget the passengers! After the Purser, the Chief Officer was the last line of defence for the Captain. A good Chief Officer was worth his weight in gold, especially to the line's senior Captains.

Will possessed all the necessary qualifications and attributes. If anything he was probably over qualified as a Chief Officer. Chief Officer on the top Cunard steamer was certainly a good position, but it was not the position that he wanted. Here he was at the age of 42 with all the necessary certificates under his belt, having served eight years as Chief Officer, yet his one ambition still eluded him; command of a crack Cunarder.

But all of these thoughts and feelings would have to wait till later to be explored. The day after Will Turner sailed out of Liverpool bound for New York on the *Lucania*, his father died; and there was no way to let him know until he returned.

Charles Turner was 73 when he died. He had commanded his first ship, *Queen of Nations* in 1870 when he was 43. His final command had been the Cunard steamer, *Cherbourg* in 1884 at the age of 57.

Charles was survived by his wife Charlotte, daughter Annie Maria and son William Thomas. Charles' career had not been spectacular, but it was certainly good. The one blemish on his record was in 1863 when his Master's certificate was suspended for six months. Despite a search at London's Guildhall Library, where the original registers of ship's captains are kept, we were unable to ascertain the reason for this suspension, as it is not recorded on Charles' original papers. His career spanned some 40 odd years and he saw sail giving way steam. He was buried in a plot of land that Will had purchased for the Turner family in the cemetery at Rake Lane, Wirral, Merseyside.

The year 1902 was a busy year and for Cunard and the Admiralty, it was a worrying one. An American Banker by the name of J. Pierpoint Morgan was able to purchase most of the transatlantic shipping lines. Having done so, he formed them into the International Mercantile Marine Company, known as the I.M.M. His acquisitions included the White Star Line, the Leyland Line, two German lines and the Dominion Line. He already owned the American Line.

Cunard were able to fend off Morgan's take over bid, though it had been a narrow squeak. The Admiralty were very concerned that with so much tonnage now under one man's control, would they still have their 'reserve forces' in the event of a national emergency? Kaiser Wilhelm of Germany had just begun rattling his sabre in pursuit of his "Weltpolitik" (World Policy). The "great naval race", an Anglo-German arms race based on naval supremacy, had begun.

The Admiralty decided to leave nothing to chance. Once more the "Special Relationship" came into play. The Admiralty and Cunard entered into intense negotiations that would secure the futures of both parties. The final outcome was a remarkable agreement, the full details of which are still secret to this day. But one thing it most definitely meant was that Cunard and the Admiralty were now inextricably intertwined.

Cunard Captain…

By the end of 1903, Will's ambition was moved one step nearer to its fulfilment. In April of that year, somebody at Cunard decided to give this man the chance to show what he was worth. Perhaps it had something to do with Will being awarded the transport medal for government service in the Boer war, who knows? The first round of medals went to a few select officers and he was included in those.

Whatever the reason, Will was promoted to the rank of Cunard Captain and on April 17th 1903 he took the bridge of the *Aleppo*, the little steamer he knew of old on the Mediterranean service.

1903 was also the year that Cunard and the British government finalised their negotiations. Under this agreement, Cunard guaranteed to remain a British company, and in the event of war to place the entire Cunard fleet at the disposal of the Admiralty. The government would loan Cunard the sum of £2,600,000 at an interest rate of a mere two and three-quarter percent over 20 years. Over those 20 years, the Admiralty would pay Cunard an *ANNUAL* subsidy of £150,000 *IN ADDITION* to all other subsidies. The crowning glory and main purpose of the loan was that Cunard would build two new ships. They were to be capable of maintaining 24 knots, mounting 12 six-inch guns and were to be the largest and fastest passenger liners on the North Atlantic, if not in the world. Cunard were to defer to the Admiralty on all questions of basic design and construction. They were to be powered solely by turbine engines giving 78,000 horsepower. They would become the *Lusitania* and the *Mauretania*.

So after 11 years as Chief Officer, Cunard, some might have said almost grudgingly, gave Will Turner a command. Not the prestigious North Atlantic, but the "backwater" service; bi-monthly to the Mediterranean. This didn't matter to Will. He had finally been given a ship of his own and would soon show them what he, "Bowler Bill" was made of.

Captain William Thomas Turner – 1903

Part of Will's "problem" was that he lacked the social airs and graces that Cunard expected of the men who captained their crack liners. Will certainly wasn't coarse or vulgar in any way, but he had a thick Liverpool accent and his manner was usually bordering on gruff. He was a sea Captain of the old school, a martinet of the days of sail. Nowadays, a captain had to be something of a hotel manager as well as a ship's master and it was not in his nature. Certainly, he could turn on the charm when necessary, usually with startling effect. But he found the world of first class passengers rather supercilious, and was unimpressed by their material wealth. They expected to be pandered to, they clamoured to sit at his table, and they expected him to return the attention. Will would have none of it. He avoided the social rituals like dinner at the Captain's table whenever he could by taking his meals on the bridge. In Will's opinion first class passengers tended to be "a load of bloody monkeys;" constantly chattering.

The other side to his "problem" was his terribly outspoken nature, coupled with a keen desire for the truth in all things. More "flexible" Captains climbed the ladder sooner. Will's friends tended to be fellow Cunard officers. Friends like Jim Watt, Daniel "Fairweather" Dow or Arthur Rostron all advised him to be a little more politic when dealing with Cunard's senior management. But it was not Will's way and Cunard did not want their customers upset by his often-brusque nature. So he was put on the Mediterranean run where, it was felt, he could do no harm.

But the board of Cunard were not prepared for Will's extraordinary character. The very personality traits which Cunard were trying to shield their customers from were having quite the opposite effect on them.

Because Will avoided them, his rare appearances at dinner in the first class dining suite became an event. Because he did not openly court their attentions, they actively sought his. The very impression of aloofness that he gave them, brought them flocking to his ship. In no time at all, he was the talk of the passengers on the Mediterranean service, because here was a Captain who was totally different. The Cunard reservations staff was now regularly being asked, "On which ship is Captain Turner next sailing and are there any passenger vacancies?"

Baffled by the phenomenon, Cunard gave him command of the *Carpathia* for the whole of 1904. Suddenly this ordinarily unremarkable ship began drawing attention to herself. She was always the fastest to "turnaround" in port. She became almost the smartest ship in the whole Cunard fleet and her crew were totally dedicated to their Captain.

37

Just in case it was a fluke, Cunard transferred Will in March 1905 to the *Ivernia* on the Boston service. Once again, the same phenomenon occurred. Cunard kept him as *Ivernia*'s Captain for the next two and a half years. Passenger revenue for the Boston service soon showed a marked improvement.

In September of 1907 another phenomenon occurred. Will's friend, Captain James Watt, was the line's Commodore and, as was the custom, took the line's newest ship on her maiden voyage. Unfortunately, due to bad weather, the new ship did not wrest the coveted Blue Riband from the Norddeutscher-Lloyd's *Kaiser Wilhelm II*, as was expected. But on her second voyage Captain Jim Watt showed the world just what Cunard's new steed was capable of. He took the record at an average speed of 23.99 knots and reduced the Atlantic crossing to under five days. The word on everyone's lips was now, "*Lusitania*".

But the world of the *Lusitania* was still a little way off for Will Turner. At the same time as the *Lusitania* was capturing the headlines, Will was transferred again. He was appointed to the *Caronia*. At least he was back on the main New York service and in command of a vessel of 19,700 tons, capable of 18 knots. Though larger than the old *Lucania*, *Caronia* was markedly slower. Not for her the title, "Ocean Greyhound", but there were other ways to make her a smart ship. And Will soon found them.

It was about this time that Will Turner met a woman by the name of Mabel Every. By this time, Will's marriage had broken down irretrievably. He and his wife were now estranged, she and the boys staying in the marital home in Manchester, Will having now moved out. Having done so, he had advertised for the services of a housekeeper.

Mabel was at that time in her early twenties, she was tall and slim with an outgoing nature. Born in Devon, she was the daughter of an army Captain who, upon his retirement, had become the Governor of Dartmoor prison. After qualifying as a nurse Mabel had seen and answered Will's advertisement and she now arrived in Liverpool to

38

take up the post. Over the years, she and Will would become inseparable.

Lusitania

On June 1st 1908, Will was appointed to Captain another of his old ships, the *Umbria*. This appointment lasted only four months for in November, Commodore James Watt retired. The new Commodore of the Cunard Line was Captain John Pritchard, who was currently serving on the *Lusitania's* sister ship, the brand new *Mauretania*. So with Will's record now speaking volumes for itself, plus a recommendation from Jim Watt, the board of Cunard finally overcame their inertia. On November 11th 1908, Captain William Thomas Turner assumed command of the *Lusitania*.

At the time of her maiden voyage in 1907, the *Lusitania* was a mammoth. She was 790 feet long overall and 87 feet wide. She carried 563 passengers first class, 464 passengers second class and 1,138 in third class or "steerage" as it was more popularly known. To drive her across the Atlantic burned 850 tons of coal every day and although she was registered at 31,550 gross tons, her actual displacement and therefore her true weight was just less than 45,000 tons. In her day she was the world's largest ship, the world's fastest liner and the largest moving object to be built by man. To accommodate her and her sister ship, the *Mauretania*, the Mersey docks had to have over 200,000 tons of sand removed from the areas adjacent to the Princes landing stage and the stage itself had to have platforms built upon it so that the gangways would reach.

Under Will Turner's command the *Lusitania* started beating her own records. *Mauretania* under Captain Pritchard soon showed herself to be slightly the faster of the two sisters. But Will and *Lusitania* did once manage to snatch the Blue Riband back from her sister. In July of 1909 though, Pritchard and *Mauretania* took it back again with a speed of 26.89 knots which Will and *Lusitania* almost equalled but could certainly never exceed. The world's press soon dubbed the Blue Riband an inter-Cunard trophy, much to the detriment and annoyance of the Germans who had nothing to compare with Cunard's two flyers.

During the crucial early days of the so-called inter-Cunard competition, Will had forged a close friendship with *Lusitania's* Chief

Engineering Officer, Archibald Bryce. Just as Will had been following in his father's footsteps, so too had Archie. His father had been an engineer with Cunard almost from the very beginning and Archie soon developed a love and that certain "feel" for steam engines, just as Will had developed that same "feel" for the ship itself. Together these two men were a winning combination because both instinctively understood their respective fields as some men are reputed to "know" horses.

Over the next seven years, Archie was to become more than just a friend to Will; he was a confidant too. It was to Archie that Will would talk about the personal side of his life. Archie in turn respected his friend's confidences. He never abused the rapport they shared at work. Archie was a very good friend to have, personally and professionally.

The Board of Cunard were not slow to notice that with Will Turner pacing the bridge and Archie Bryce heading the engine room, the *Lusitania* ran like clockwork. She always looked her best and the whole crew took great pride in their ship and their Captain. She was every inch the crack liner she was built to be. Cunard had to admit it, they'd been wrong about Will Turner. From now on, they'd treat him differently.

In December of 1909, Commodore Pritchard retired. As part of Cunard's new policy of treating Will Turner differently, they appointed him to succeed Pritchard; not as Commodore, but as Captain of the *Mauretania*, which at that moment was in dry dock undergoing her annual overhaul. The man who was to take Will's place commanding the *Lusitania* was a friend of his, Captain James T. Charles, whom Will had known since they served together on the *Lucania*. Will was now sufficiently placed to put a small condition upon his acceptance. Archie Bryce was to transfer with him. Cunard readily agreed and on January 27th, 1910 Will Turner took *Mauretania* out of Liverpool a very happy Captain.

On 2nd September that year, there occurred a piece of high drama involving Captain Turner, the *Mauretania* and the crew of another Liverpool ship, the *West Point*.

41

Archie Bryce - Chief Engineer

On 29th August at 18.00 hours, the *West Point* had sunk in the North Atlantic, following an uncontrollable fire on board. She carried no passengers, but her Master, Captain James Pinkham and his crew had now been adrift on the open ocean in lifeboats for six whole days. A passing steamer, the *Devonian*, had sighted and picked up the occupants of one of the lifeboats not too long after the *West Point* had foundered, but at the time, there was no sign of the Captain and the 15 other members of the crew who were still missing. *Devonian* had put out a wireless call, which was answered by the *Mauretania*, and Captain Turner promptly diverted his ship and began a search for them. But the weather had turned bad and a high sea was running. Nobody held out much hope for the missing men.

By the time Will Turner found them, Captain Pinkham and the remaining members of his crew had all but given up hope. However, Will Turner was not about to abandon his fellow seamen to their fate. He was determined to rescue them, despite the weather, and he very skillfully manoeuvred the *Mauretania* to within a few yards of their lifeboat. Using every means possible, the *West Point's* boat was recovered safely, and a most grateful Captain Pinkham and his crew were successfully rescued. Will Turner later received an illuminated address from the Liverpool Shipwreck and Humane Society, for his masterly display of ship handling.

Given that Will now had command of the faster of Cunard's flagships, it was only natural that he should better the records he'd set with the *Lusitania*. This he did. The crossings were quicker and so also the time taken to turn the ship around in port.

With this factor uppermost in their minds, the board of Cunard made a startling announcement at the beginning of December, 1910. The *Mauretania* under Captain Turner was to make a "Christmas Special" round voyage. Liverpool to New York and then back in just 12 days. There were many people, experts among them, who said that it couldn't possibly be done. For one thing, the weather would be against it; the Atlantic was notorious for being angry in winter plus the fact that it normally took three to five days to turn the ship around in New York. Coaling alone could easily account for three days.

Cunard's plan was that, Westbound; *Mauretania* would be taking American citizens who perhaps lived in England, home in time to spend Christmas with their families. On the return journey, it would be Britons and perhaps Western Europeans who would be coming home for Christmas. To hasten the passengers' journey on the return trip, *Mauretania* would call at Fishguard, where special trains laid on by Cunard would speed the passengers to London. The

43

schedule of 12 days for the entire round voyage meant that the maximum time *Mauretania* could take to turn round in New York was a mere 48 hours. Having widely publicised the event, Cunard had more or less put their reputation on the line, as journalists from most of the leading national newspapers would also be aboard for the entire voyage, which was scheduled to leave Liverpool on the evening of Saturday, December 10th.

At a little after 17:40 hours on the appointed day, *Mauretania* left the Prince's landing stage having embarked 1,280 passengers for the epic voyage. Will Turner was on the bridge but the Chief Engineer for this trip was John Kendall, not Archie Bryce, who was on leave.

From the outset, the weather was certainly against them. The Daily Mail's correspondent sent his report by wireless and he described the voyage as "eventful and tempestuous", with the barometer reading as low as 28.18 at one stage, the sea temperature at freezing point and the *Mauretania* having passed through six snow storms in one day. The wind was Westerly and gale force in strength and the seas were described as "tumbling". With weather conditions such as these, Will had no option but to reduce speed. Most of the passengers spent the voyage in their cabins.

In the early morning of Friday December 15th, Will brought *Mauretania* into New York harbour, some 18 hours later than was originally planned. The weather was so cold that the entire ship was coated in frost. Icicles clung to her rigging, giving her the appearance of having been especially decorated for the festive Season. They now had an absolute maximum of 30 hours in which to turn her around if she was to re-cross the Atlantic in time to meet the special trains at Fishguard.

The whole ship's crew, the postal clerks, the New York dock workers and the Cunard staff in New York, worked frantically to refuel, provision and victual the ship. The embarking passengers were processed in record time by U.S. Customs officials, as was the freight and baggage. The result was that they beat the deadline: Just!

At 18:00 hours precisely on Saturday, December 16th, the

Cunard Marine Superintendent for the port of New York, Captain Roberts, flashed the "all is clear" signal from the outer end of the pier. The signal was repeated by a man standing on the roof of the pier to Will Turner on the *Mauretania*'s bridge. Will then rang "stand by" on the main engine telegraphs. The mooring lines were cast off and assisted by three tugs, *Mauretania* backed slowly away from her berth. The tugs cast her off in midstream as soon as they had turned her and the minute they were clear, Will rang down to the engine room for "slow ahead".

Watchers lined the waterfront to see her off. As her massive turbines came to life, Will sounded off the whistle in farewell. The gesture was returned by just about every ship and boat in the harbour. Even the tugs joined in to give her the noisiest of send offs.

The return passage was accompanied by good weather and *Mauretania* was able to cross the Atlantic at an average speed of 25.07 knots. She landed mails and some of her passengers during a brief stop at Queenstown, Ireland, and then at midnight on Thursday, December 22nd she arrived at Fishguard, where 600 passengers disembarked and left on the special trains provided by Cunard. She then returned to her home port of Liverpool.

The "Christmas Special" was an unprecedented success, if only by the narrowest of margins, but it earned for *Mauretania* the proud distinction of being the first liner to make the round voyage to New York and back in just 12 days.

On January 19th, 1911, Cunard's Board of Directors decided to present Will Turner with a silver salver to mark the occasion of the recent record voyage. Captain Roberts, the New York Cunard Superintendent and *Mauretania*'s Chief Engineer, John Kendall also received a similar presentation from the Cunard company secretary, W. Dranfield.

Shortly after this, Will wrote a letter to the Cunard chairman, Alfred Booth from his day cabin aboard the *Mauretania*. It read as follows:

Sir,

I had not time before leaving Liverpool to write to thank you most sincerely for the handsome salver which you so kindly presented to me in connection with the record voyage of the "Mauretania". I did not expect to receive any such recognition of my part in the matter. We all on board tried to do our duty as under any ordinary circumstances. It is very gratifying to know that what we did met with the approval of the company, and I shall highly prize this appreciation, and again, sir, thank you most humbly for it.

I remain, sir,

Your grateful & obedient servant

(signed) W T Turner.

Self-effacing as Will's letter undoubtedly was, it was patently obvious to Cunard that Captain Turner was a master of shiphandling as well as a superb seaman.

In June of 1911, the old rival, the White Star Line, introduced their new ship *Olympic*. With a displacement figure of nearly 66,000 tons she was the world's largest ship. But she was designed for comfort and luxury, not speed. Though she was only four knots slower than the *Mauretania*.

However, determined not to be totally outshone by the White Star Line's latest addition, the Board of Cunard announced another "Special". This time it was a "Coronation Special" starting from New York.

On June 22nd at Westminster Abbey in London, King George V and Queen Mary were due to be crowned. It was rightly anticipated by Cunard that there would be a large number of Americans eager to attend. Once more, Will Turner and the *Mauretania* were to be given the honour of performing the task.

Mauretania left New York on June 14th with a total of 2,039

46

passengers bound once again for Fishguard and the same arrangement of special trains to London. She then returned to Liverpool. On June 24th the returning Coronation tourists boarded the *Mauretania* at Liverpool, landing in New York on June 29th. It proved to be another feather in the respective caps of Cunard and Will Turner.

For December 1911, another "Christmas Special" was announced but this time, fate prevented Will Turner and the *Mauretania* from fulfiling the promise. On December 7th, 1911, just two days before the due departure date of the "Christmas Special", gale force winds struck Liverpool. *Mauretania* broke free from her moorings at the Sloyne buoy and ran aground. She had to be dry docked as a result of the damage she sustained, so Will's friend, Captain J. T. Charles and the *Lusitania*, stepped into the breach. The "Christmas Special" went ahead as planned and thanks to another lightning turnaround, the deadline was met.

In April of 1912, White Star followed *Olympic* with her sister ship, the slightly larger *Titanic*. By a coincidence of scheduling Will Turner and the *Mauretania* sailed from Liverpool on the same day that *Titanic* departed Southampton on her maiden voyage. *Titanic* had an extra stop at Cherbourg in France on her schedule so *Mauretania*, despite starting out on the same day, would be expected to arrive a good day and a half ahead of *Titanic* anyway. However, as history shows, only one of them made it across the Atlantic. *Titanic* collided with an iceberg and sank, taking with her 1,503 from the 2,207 aboard her. The survivors owed their lives to one of Will's friends, Captain Arthur Rostron of Will's old ship, the *Carpathia*. The orders, which Rostron issued during *Carpathia's* frantic 58-mile dash to *Titanic's* rescue, are today recognised as masterpiece examples of seamanship. Rostron would later go on to be a celebrated Commodore of the Cunard line himself and ended his career by being knighted.

Commodore of the Line...

If the previous two years had been notable in Will's life, then 1913 was a gala year. Still in command of Cunard's flagship the *Mauretania*, he was finally promoted to Commodore in March. He was now the Cunard Line's senior Captain, drawing a salary of £1,100 per annum.

Then in June came the news that the Admiralty had decided to confer upon him the rank of honourary Commander in the Royal Navy Reserve. In an article headlined "*Mauretania's* Captain honoured", the Journal of Commerce (Liverpool and London) observed that "Captain Turner, one may say, holds the highest and proudest position in the British Mercantile Marine..." After mentioning the Admiralty's honouring of him, and the fine reputation he had built up for himself, the Journal went on to point out that on July 11th, the King and Queen were expected aboard the *Mauretania* as part of the Mersey review. It was Will's job to conduct their Majesties on a tour of Britain's premier transatlantic liner, the *Mauretania*, after personally welcoming them aboard. The event went without a hitch and Will's reputation was assured.

The only event that cast a shadow upon this memorable year happened on November 13th. At the age of 59, his sister Annie Maria died suddenly. The funeral was again at the Rake Lane cemetery where she was laid to rest with their father, Charles, in the family grave. This time Will was able to attend and he missed the *Mauretania*'s next sailing whilst on compassionate leave.

At the end of 1913 *Mauretania* was dry docked again for her annual overhaul. Will took an extended leave and in April of 1914 he captained *Lusitania* for two round transatlantic voyages.

On May 30th, 1914, in a blaze of publicity, Commodore William Thomas Turner took Cunard's brand new, and largest ship

Cunard Commodore William Thomas Turner

yet, the *Aquitania*, out of Liverpool on her maiden voyage to New York. Once more, Archie Bryce was Chief Engineer. She was roughly the same size as the *White Star* Line's *Titanic* had been. She had not been designed as a Blue Riband contender and her top speed of 23 knots was slightly slower than that of *Mauretania*. But she was a beautiful ship and incidentally, the first Cunarder to boast a swimming pool and the last liner ever to be built with four funnels. She was also unusual in the respect that she carried a "Staff Captain". Amongst his duties, was to take the place of the Captain at the ships social events when the Captain was unavailable. He was John Anderson.

Her maiden arrival in New York, though spectacular, was later than expected and was overshadowed by the *Empress of Ireland* disaster in Canada. *Aquitania*'s time for her maiden crossing the North Atlantic was five days, 17 hours and 43 minutes. On the third day of her Atlantic passage the ship had received an ice warning and Captain Turner prudently steered his ship much further south than was usual in order to avoid the ice. This safety precaution had added almost 100 miles to *Aquitania*'s journey. Will Turner made a total of two round voyages to New York as *Aquitania*'s captain and on their third arrival, he put on something of a show by docking the huge liner without the aid of tugs, as he had often done with *Lusitania* and the *Mauretania*. With *Aquitania* though, he set a record by accomplishing the task in a mere 19 minutes. But then Will's shiphandling skills were by now becoming legendary.

On August 4th, 1914 something happened which was to change everything, permanently. The powder keg which had been smouldering for over seven years finally exploded, and the "Great War" broke out.

At this juncture we must briefly pause in the following of Will's life and career. We need to do this because both were about to be radically altered by a combination of circumstance, people and events. The trail is a complex one and to fully understand the ramifications and consequences for Will Turner, some foundations must now be laid and scenes set. We have tried to keep this to a minimum without detraction from Will's story, but key people are about to interpose and it is important to introduce them without delay as their actions, or sometimes lack of actions, had a direct bearing on Will's life in a way that could not possibly have been foreseen.

Aquitania's maiden arrival in New York

51

Your Country Needs You...

August 1914: Kaiser Wilhelm II of Germany had finally reached the point of no return. He'd been rattling his sabre at Germany's neighbours for so long now that his "Weltpolitik" would have to be backed by force. The spark caused by the assassination of Archduke Ferdinand was nothing more than an elaborate pretext for what many far-sighted individuals saw as the inevitable.

Yet surprisingly, there were still many world statesmen who shared the view that this war would be over by Christmas. Unfortunately, a secret arrangement of mutual assistance treaties, the full extent of which neither side appreciated at the time, meant that too many nations were now involved to be able to halt the runaway situation.

Germany had been preparing for this war for years. Her armies were well organised, highly trained, modern and ready. The French armies could fulfil none of those criteria. Britain's armies were better than those of France, but were still no match for the might of the German army.

Britain placed her faith in the Royal Navy, traditional guardian of these sceptred isles. The German Navy was modern, but under strength and largely untried more than anything. It was more the reputation of the Royal Navy's invincibility, which had previously governed the war plans of any foreign power.

With the quick collapse of the Belgian army following the German invasion, the French and the British found their backs well and truly against the wall. But circumstances caused the Germans to hesitate, and fatally for them, they departed from the well thought out Von Schlieffen plan. The Allies were quick to exploit this situation and suddenly the runaway steamroller of the German advance was checked. But it could not be pushed back. Stalemate ensued; trenches were dug then made more elaborate and both sides settled into the deadlock, which would last for four years. The long drawn out war of attrition, which Lord Kitchener had foreseen and been publicly derided for, now became an inescapable fact.

Before the war was even two months old, Kitchener brought another inescapable fact to the attention of senior government officials. The British Army was firing more shells per week than the armaments factories made. Reserves were already down to about a three-month supply and there was every indication of worse things to come.

So, with British factories unable to meet the demand, alternative suppliers had to be found if a crisis was to be averted. The largest of these alternative suppliers turned out to be the Bethlehem Steel Corporation in the United States. They were certainly large enough to fill the gap, but another problem now presented itself. How to get the vital munitions to England quickly? The fastest cargo ships were only capable of around twelve, possibly fourteen knots. Assuming that a German U-boat didn't sink the freighter on the way, it would still take nine days to get each shipment across the Atlantic. Nine days might suffice for the more routine items but ammunition was desperately needed.

There was a faster way, but shipping explosives on civilian passengers liners was morally unacceptable and wholly contrary to American law. Or was it?

As it transpired, two relevant loopholes in American law were discovered. In 1910, a large pile of cases containing shotgun cartridges and assorted calibre pistol ammunition had been deliberately set on fire for the benefit of the municipal explosives commission of New York city. As no physical explosion was seen to result, the commission gave their authorisation for ammunition to be shipped on public railways and passenger vessels, provided that each case of ammunition was clearly marked NON EXPLOSIVE IN BULK. The commissioners were not explosive experts and all the cartridges used in the demonstration were of the old-fashioned black powder type. Black powder would burn fiercely, but out in the open as this demonstration proved, the explosive gases this produced would diffuse into the atmosphere. Confined, it would of course have exploded. There was the first loophole.

The second loophole came in answer to the problem of getting the now supposedly non-explosive munitions onto British passenger liners. To that end it became standard practice to file a false manifest with the U.S. Collector of Customs in New York, one Mr. Dudley Field Malone. Malone would issue the sailing clearance certificate on the basis of a manifest, which showed only a general cargo. Once the ship was safely at sea and outside of U.S. territorial waters, a 'supplementary' manifest would then be filed listing all "last minute" provisions taken on board and any obviously contraband goods would be disguised as seemingly innocent items like "machine parts", or "metallic packages", or large packages of cheese or butter. Malone knew the probable nature of the items but was instructed to turn a blind eye to it.

Having got round these two obstacles, the British Government ran into a logistics problem. The sheer quantities involved were bound to show up on U.S. records somewhere. America's president, Woodrow Wilson, had declared a policy of strict neutrality. America could not afford to be publicly seen as England's arms supplier.

The answer lay in one man: Mr John Pierpoint Morgan, the eminent American banker and the very man whose earlier actions had caused the Admiralty and Cunard such consternation with his formation of the I.M.M. Company. As it transpired, Morgan's sympathies were entirely with the Allied cause.

The British Government enlisted him to act as a central purchasing and shipping agent for these illicit supplies. Having most of the Atlantic shipping lines under his control, plus the huge resources of the Morgan bank, he was ideally placed and more than willing. He also had no scruples, which was a great attribute in his line of work.

Morgan was left to make all the necessary arrangements. He set up a complex chain of fictitious companies with corresponding bank accounts. He needed these to legitimise the purchases he was making on behalf of the British Government. Then I.M.M.'s ships and passengers would be the unwitting carriers, ably assisted by any British civilian ships, which the Admiralty had control over or could charter. The arrangements at the British end were left to the Admiralty's trade division, under Captain Richard Webb. The trade division also prepared the Admiralty advices and notices to mariners, which all merchant navy Captains were given for their guidance.

The final two people who need mentioning here are Jacky Fisher and Winston Churchill. The first named was a retired Admiral and visionary. Under his tenure the Royal Navy had progressed in leaps and bounds. It was his foresight alone that had led to the development of such warships as the revolutionary *Dreadnought*. He had nurtured his navy, often against stiff opposition, and made it what it was in 1914. "The police force of the empire", it had once been called; Fisher liked that. But Fisher had his faults and paranoia was one of them. He was what might today be called a "control freak". He was obsessed with a need for total secrecy that, unfortunately, often lead to crucial intelligence being suppressed or otherwise failing to reach the people who really needed it immediately. In 1915, he was also 75 years of age and sadly suffering badly from senility and delusions of his own importance. As far as he was concerned, the only right way was his way. You were either for him or against him, and if you were against him, he would do his utmost to destroy you, in which he usually succeeded.

Winston Churchill was a politician. He'd chosen the Admiralty in 1911 because it offered the best chance of publicity. He held the position of first Lord of the Admiralty whilst Fisher was first Sea Lord. This arrangement made them joint commanders of the Admiralty. The Royal Navy was popular with the people of Britain. It has always been a great British institution. Over the preceding ten years, a great deal of public money and attention had been lavished upon it and it was the finest battle fleet in the world; but then it had to be. Both Fisher and Churchill calculated that sooner or later a decisive naval battle was bound to take place, another Trafalgar. If such was the case, Churchill was determined to be most prominently associated with it. Oh yes, the Admiralty looked very promising to young Winston.

Churchill and Fisher started out as the best of friends, but as Churchill settled in and gradually ran the Admiralty his way, they started to clash. The two men had totally different working patterns and Churchill was apt to disappear, often at critical times, in furtherance of his own personal aims. This left the ageing Fisher to cope single-handedly and he greatly resented it. By May 1915, Churchill and Fisher's relationship had deteriorated to the point where it could only be described as acrimonious, chiefly due to Churchill's disastrous Dardanelles operation and Fisher's total opposition to it.

Such then were the background scenes. Over the next nine months, as we shall see, fate had a lot in store for most of the participants, which culminated one day in May of 1915, when to quote Thomas Hardy's poem about the *Titanic* disaster, Convergence of the Twain; "The spinner of the years says now! Each one hears and consummation comes, and jars two hemispheres".

The most immediate consequence for Will Turner of the declaration of war was that in common with a few of the other senior Cunard Captains; he was temporarily without a ship. As soon as *Lusitania*, *Mauretania* and *Aquitania* were back in Liverpool, they were instantly requisitioned for government service under the terms of the 1903 agreement, for use as auxiliary cruisers. The crews were reassigned to other ships. However, it was decided (after Admiralty refitting of the ships) that each was unsuitable for use as a cruiser by virtue of being too large and consuming too much fuel.

Mauretania and *Aquitania* were retained by the Admiralty for use as troopships. *Lusitania*, much modified, was returned to Cunard in September of 1914. The Admiralty told Cunard to put the *Lusitania* back into the North Atlantic service, but with conditions imposed on her use. Certain sections of the ship were now to be reserved for the sole use of the Admiralty's trade department. If any spaces were left over on eastbound crossings, Cunard could utilise them subject to permission from the Admiralty.

56

During her Admiralty refit, *Lusitania* was fitted with the mountings for her complement of six-inch guns. These mountings were concealed beneath the deck planking. The guns themselves, though ordered, were never actually fitted. But by far the biggest alteration that was made to her was the removal of all the passenger accommodation, mainly third class, in the forward sections between the first coalbunker and the bows. This was now made into additional cargo space. In this condition she was returned to Cunard, who were also told that all cargo carried in this new space would be specially insured by the British Government. In addition, the deployment and navigation of the *Lusitania* was now the Admiralty's responsibility, not Cunard's. In short, Cunard was now under the command of the Admiralty.

The *Lusitania* returned to a monthly Atlantic run in October of 1914 under her regular Captain, Daniel Dow, known to his friends (Will Turner included) as "Fairweather". He had been given this nickname as he displayed a tendency toward seasickness! He was therefore deemed to be an expert in smooth crossings. Archie Bryce was also reappointed as her Chief Engineering Officer.

For Will, other consequences of the war now presented themselves. His two sons, Norman and Percy, both joined up. Norman became a commissioned officer in the Royal Artillery and quickly found himself serving on the Western front. Percy followed in his father's footsteps and joined the merchant navy.

With the munitions crisis deepening and the last kinks being ironed out of the J.P. Morgan/ Admiralty/ British Government supply line; ships were urgently needed to convey these precious cargoes Eastbound across the Atlantic. In 1914, Scott's of Greenock built a new ship for Cunard. She was a 14,315-ton liner by the name of *Transylvania*. She was fairly small by the standard for recent Cunard passenger ships, being 548 feet long with a beam of 66 feet. She was designed along the precedent set by *Lusitania* as she was powered by four direct drive steam turbines, driving twin screws. One curious fact about her is that although you can find her in the 1914/1915 Lloyds register of shipping, and she is listed as being built for, and owned by Cunard, you won't find her listed in Cunard's fleet index in "Merchant fleets in profile", by Duncan Haws. This is a curious omission to say the least, as "Merchant fleets in profile" is a commonly used reference publication.

Be that as it may, on December 4th, 1914, Cunard's newest ship, the *Transylvania*, sailed unostentatiously on her "maiden voyage" to America under the command of Cunard's Commodore, Captain William Thomas Turner, who was glad to have a ship again.

As 1914 gave way to 1915, it became obvious that the war was not going to be of the quick and decisive kind. Lord Kitchener's forecast of a long, drawn out affair was becoming a reality. In February of 1915, Great Britain declared a Naval blockade of Germany, thus beginning a policy for starvation of the raw materials that Germany needed. The Germans responded to this action by declaring the waters around the British Isles to be a war zone and stepping up the operations of their U-boats against British and allied shipping. Measure was followed by counter measure; British ships flew neutral flags and were given Admiralty instructions to ram U-boats.

Up to this point, German U-boats had been following the "Cruiser rules" with regard to attacking merchant shipping. These rules required U-boat commanders to surface, fire a warning shot across a ship's bow then board and search the vessel. If found to be a British vessel or one carrying supplies for the Allies, then time was given for the crew to man the lifeboats and abandon ship. The ship was then torpedoed, or sunk by gunfire.

However, once it was discovered that British merchant ships now had Admiralty instructions to counter attack U-boats, the cruiser rules were discarded.

This was in fact exactly the situation which Winston Churchill, First Lord of the Admiralty, had striven to achieve. In a secret letter to Walter Runciman, the President of the Board of Trade, he had written:

"My Dear Walter,

It is most important to attract neutral shipping to our shores, in the hope especially of embroiling the U.S. with Germany. The German formal announcement of indiscriminate submarine attacks has been made to the United States to produce a deterrent effect upon traffic. ....for our part we want the traffic - , the more the better. And if some of it gets into trouble, better still".

(signed) W.S. Churchill.

Churchill hoped that the U-boat commanders would be goaded into attacking ANY ship in British waters. Ultimately of course, they would be bound to attack a neutral ship, hopefully an American one. By following a policy aimed at deliberately embroiling America with Germany, Churchill hoped to bring America into the war on the side of the British. Unfortunately Churchill either did not realise, or did not care, that America was physically incapable of going to war in 1915, even if she desired it. Her standing armies were too small for war on such a scale and would require nearly two years to reach the strength needed. But far more importantly for the British, if America declared war in 1915, Britain's source of munitions would dry up, as priority would have been given to America's armed forces, which had only limited stocks. Fortunately for the allies, far more astute Statesmen than Churchill were in charge. American neutrality was upheld, munitions supplies were maintained and Churchill was kept in check. But Churchill was a dangerous man, and his frustrations were starting to simmer.

February 1915 also saw Will Turner bringing the *Transylvania* back across the Atlantic from America in company with another Cunarder, the *Ausonia*. The German U-boat *U-21* had caused alarm by sinking three ships in broad daylight in Liverpool bay on January 30th. *U-21* then started her voyage home, which brought her into the waters of the Atlantic Ocean off Ireland's South coast.

Transylvania and *Ausonia* were also expected in those same waters at the same time. The Admiralty took no chances. Both ships were sent a message diverting them into Queenstown harbour, there to wait protected by the harbour's anti submarine boom, for a destroyer escort for the last leg of the journey to Liverpool. Though by no means famous liners the *Transylvania* and *Ausonia* had to be safeguarded at all costs. This was not so much due to any concern the Admiralty had for the safety of the passengers, but was due to the fact that each ship had a 14inch gun lashed to it's foredeck. The guns weighed 70 tons each and had been made by the Bethlehem Steel Corporation of America and sold to the Royal Navy.

Steaming behind *Transylvania* and *Ausonia* came the *Lusitania* under Captain Dow. When informed of the U-boat peril, Dow ran up the Stars and Stripes and bolted for Liverpool. The incident did not pass unnoticed, and there were diplomatic repercussions. However, political oil was poured onto the troubled American waters and no more was said, but it was a measure of the strain Captain Dow was feeling. By the end of the first week in March of 1915, the strain finally proved to be too much. Captain Dow had yet to see a German U-boat but his continuing fear of being torpedoed, given that he knew something of the nature of his cargo, caused him to worry greatly about the safety of his passengers.

Alfred Booth, the chairman of Cunard decided that Captain Dow needed a rest. He searched his list of Cunard Captains for a suitable replacement master. He stopped looking when his eyes fell on the name of Turner, William Thomas. "Of course," he thought to himself, " Thank God for Captain Turner."

His appointment confirmed, Will inspected the *Lusitania* thoroughly on March 10th 1915. He found a good deal at fault. However, on the premise that there was a war on; he took the *Lusitania* to New York on March 16th.

Upon his return however, he was an angry and worried man. Having consulted with Archie Bryce, he sat down at home and wrote a scathing report to Alfred Booth, regarding the state of his former ship. He found the turbine engines in need of attention, the standard of the crew's seamanship left much to be desired, some of the lifesaving equipment was defective and that the ship could not be properly ballasted due to defective trim tanks. He also discovered, by way of

Archie Bryce, that on Captain Dow's last trip, the "government people" in New York had managed to fill the *Lusitania's* double bottoms with 100,000 gallons of diesel fuel, and that one boiler room had been shut down to economise on coal.

Not content with voicing his opinions to Alfred Booth, Will also reported the defects to the Board of Trade Surveyor in Liverpool. He did not mention the diesel to the surveyor, but he did tell Alfred Booth that unless the defects were rectified he would not take the *Lusitania* out again.

A few days later Alfred Booth visited Will in his spacious day cabin aboard the *Lusitania*, which he noticed was already looking more like her pre-war self, to discuss Will's report. He had heard of Captain Turner's legendary obstinacy but up till now, he'd never encountered it on a personal basis. Dealing with each point in Will's report, Booth explained that the Royal Navy had taken the best men quite early on in the war. Every effort was being made to provide good men for the *Lusitania*, but it was not always possible, which was why nearly every voyage was made with a scratch crew, and those signing on as stewards were apt to desert in New York.

Booth went on to explain that due to falling passenger demand and the price of coal, one boiler room had indeed been shut down, to save money. This also meant that Archie Bryce's engineering department were short of the 90 men required to man the closed boiler room, a further saving. However, like Captain Dow before him, Will managed to successfully argue for a full coal supply anyway, which although the ship did not actually need it, would at least solve the worst of the ballasting problem. Cunard's accounts department had previously discovered that coal was substantially cheaper in the United States, so in future *Lusitania's* bunkers would be filled to capacity each time she was in New York.

Booth wanted to postpone any work on the turbine engines for as long as he possibly could. Working on the engines invariably caused long delays and he was running to a tight Admiralty schedule, though he did not share that information with Will, who was consistently arguing on the grounds of passenger safety, particularly now that there was a war on. It was Cunard's proud claim that they'd never lost a life, and Will was using that very claim to counter Booth's objections, using the Board of Trade Surveyor as an additional lever. Booth found the discussion heavy going and finally conceded, though only the most pressing repairs were to be carried out. The rest would have to wait till *Lusitania's* scheduled refit.

Alfred Booth – Cunard Chairman

On the question of the lifesaving equipment, the Board of Trade Surveyor's decision was final. It resulted in the replacement of three of the lifeboats.

The only defect that couldn't be remedied was in the engine room. Due to faulty valves in the supply lines to the low pressure turbines, "Full Astern" could not be selected in an emergency as the resulting steam pressure would place too great a strain on the valves, which would subsequently blow out.

After a long and arduous discussion, Will realised that he had got most of what he'd wanted. Booth had an appointment in London and was now pressed for time. He could not believe that he had spent so long arguing, arguing, with one of his Captains. It was maddening in the extreme. He was not used to getting as good as he gave and certainly not from an employee. What was it about this man Turner?

As Booth anxiously checked his watch again, he looked up at Will and later recalled seeing it. The eyes! That was what did it. They were of a vivid, penetrating blue, which held one transfixed. You could not escape them.

Rising to leave, Booth noticed that there were two hats on the back of the cabin door. The first was the white topped peaked cap with gold braided visor of the Cunard Commodore. The other was a bowler hat. As the two men walked out of the day cabin and headed toward the main lifts, Booth noticed that Turner had instinctively taken the bowler. "Bowler Bill, so it was true," he thought to himself.

On the way to the lift, Will managed one last concession from Booth. On the grounds of the reduced crew and the fact that he would have to spend most of his time on the bridge, due to the submarine threat, the post of Staff Captain was to be reinstated, as on the *Aquitania*. Will asked for John Anderson again and Booth granted the request as the lift arrived. As the lift started down, Booth was struck by another thought which was, "like him or loathe him, but one had to admire him." Fortunately, Booth happened to like Will as well as admire him, which was to stand Will in good stead at a later date.

On April 17th 1915, her defects remedied, (apart from the valves on the low pressure turbines) *Lusitania* sailed from Liverpool bound for New York. Mabel Every came to see her off and recalled that it was Staff Captain John Anderson who was on the bridge to take her out. Will Turner, sporting a brand new bowler hat, was up on the forecastle admonishing the Bosun for his apparently lethargic windlass crew.

An Englishman in New York...

T he Westbound voyage to New York was uneventful and *Lusitania* arrived there on the morning of April 24th. Coming off the Atlantic into Lower Bay, brought her into the Hudson River, with Staten Island and Liberty Island (with its famous Statue of Liberty) to port. *Lusitania* would pass Battery Park on her starboard side, she would then pass the Cunard piers, turn round in mid river and dock at pier 54. Will docked her unaided, though in nothing like his record time of 19 minutes, then left Staff Captain Anderson to see to the formalities and the unloading. There was not much unloading to do on the westbound crossing and they had nothing like a full complement of passengers.

After a snack lunch in his day cabin and a quick discussion with Archie Bryce, Will went ashore. He loved New York; it was such a vibrant place and he seldom got the chance to just walk about the city, so whenever an opportunity arose he took it. Besides which, he knew she would be waiting for him, as she always was. Her name was Mercedes Desmore and she always knew when he was coming. But then again, just about everybody in New York knew when the *Lusitania* was in.

New York differed in almost every respect to any other place outside the United States that Will had visited. The system of unusually wide avenues and streets that criss-crossed the city and led to such ethnic districts as Chinatown, little Italy and Greenwich Village, fascinated him. Settlers from all over the world had set up their own little communities in New York. Wall Street was emerging as a financial centre of the world. Huge department stores and restaurants with themes from Europe, Asia and all corners of the globe were found in abundance. New York was the gateway to a new world for thousands of immigrants and those that came were welcomed by the statue of Liberty towering over the entrance to the harbour.

Mercedes Desmore

Theatre played a big part in New York life. Theatre land was set around Times Square and Broadway and actors and actresses from all over the world made for the area seeking fame and fortune. Will Turner's niece, Mercedes Desmore, was a part of that community. She was at that time appearing at the New Amsterdam Theatre in the Henry Arthur Jones play, "THE LIE." Will adored his niece and would spend what little spare time he had ashore with Mercedes.

66

Mercedes had gone to New York after retiring from her stage career in England, which had seen her play alongside such people as Ellen Terry, Lewis Waller, George Grossmith and Sir Herbert Tree. Her whole life had seemed as though it had been spent in the theatre and she wanted a change, to be "domesticated" as she put it. After a time in America and away from the theatre, her friends persuaded her to go back on stage, one even offered to sponsor her. Mercedes, who appeared to be taking the whole thing as a joke, agreed. After a meeting with a local theatre company manager (he thought he had made a rare find), she was offered a contract. Before she put her name to it she revealed her theatrical career in England. A new contract was hastily drawn up with a far better salary and conditions, to which Mercedes then signed. Her desire for histrionic work had returned. She went on to have a long and distinguished career in America.

Whilst in New York, Will had some business to attend to on the day before his departure, on behalf of Cunard, which pertained to their great rival, the White Star Line. White Star were seeking to limit their liability for the loss of the *Titanic*. As Commodore of the Cunard Line, Will was to make a statement about how these large liners were operated. The statement, made before a notary, was to be read in court. One of the points the court wished to cover was the issuing of binoculars to lookouts. It had transpired that the lookouts in *Titanic*'s crows nest that fateful night did not have any and some thought that if they had, possibly the iceberg would have been seen earlier and therefore perhaps, disaster averted.

The notary asked Will if the lookouts on the *Lusitania* were issued with binoculars. "Certainly not," Will replied, "might as well give them soda bottles for all the good it will do."

Will then gave some brief details as to the layout of *Lusitania's* watertight bulkheads and just before he left, the notary asked him a question, off the record. The notary asked him if he had personally learned anything from the *Titanic* disaster, particularly with regard to Captain Smith apparently steaming at full speed into a known icefield. "I did not learn the slightest thing from that accident," Will told him. "It could happen again."

This last piece of dialogue has often been used in the light of subsequent events, to illustrate Will Turner's supposed intransigence. Will's attitude was exactly the same as any other senior Captain of his day. The long established custom in the crack passenger liners of this era was to proceed at full speed once on the open ocean, and not slacken the pace unless bad weather or a physical danger, such as an iceberg, was actually encountered. Nobody today would deny that this was a bad custom to say the least, but there is absolutely no point in judging those Captains by today's standards. They can only be judged by the standards of their own day. Today, some of their practices would perhaps be considered as bordering on negligent navigation, but in the era we are dealing with here, these were certainly the accepted practices of the day, which is a fact that we must both acknowledge and accept when we consider their actions.

Having made his statement, Will then left to go to the Customs house with the manifest for the *Lusitania's* trip home. That done, he left the Customs house and made for his usual port of call when in New York, a restaurant on 14th street called Luchow's. It was a German restaurant founded in 1882 by Guido August Luchow, and was frequented by most of the Captains of the crack transatlantic liners. As holder of the Blue Riband with *Mauretania*, Will was respected by the German Captains, from whom Cunard had taken the honour. But their respect was tempered with hatred.

History now tells us that Will and Mercedes would not see the *Lusitania* docked in New York again. The next voyage, bound for Liverpool, would be her last. Fate, misfortune, the exigencies of war, and incompetence would ensure that history recorded her final resting place as eleven and a quarter miles off the Old Head of Kinsale, Southern Ireland.

Those whole six days that *Lusitania* was in port had been spent in preparation for her departure on Saturday, May 1st. The biggest job was coaling, and that was started within three hours of her arrival. Coal lighters were moored all along her port side and the coal started to be loaded via special apertures in her side. It was a long, laborious and above all filthy job and the ship would have to be thoroughly cleaned afterwards.

There was also the cargo to be loaded, most of which was urgent government consignments though the manifest of course would tell a different story. Then there was the passengers' baggage. The responsibility for all the loading arrangements lay with Staff Captain John Anderson and he duly delegated the responsibility for the passengers' luggage to the ship's new junior Third Officer, Albert Bestic. Bestic had only joined the ship that week in New York prior to her May 1st departure. He was a last minute replacement for *Lusitania's* previous junior Third. Upon joining the ship, he presented himself to Captain Turner on the bridge. Bestic had two uniforms. One was his best and the other was what he called his working uniform. He'd not had time to change and therefore stood somewhat apprehensively in front of the line's Commodore, looking less than resplendent. Bestic had stood rigidly to attention as his Captain looked him up and down, taking in the fact that although the uniform had been cleaned, there were still obvious signs of it's service; the odd small grease mark, and a snag here and there.

Bestic was expecting to be bawled out at any moment over his appearance. Instead, Will simply asked him in a firm but level tone what his name was. "Bestic, sir" he replied. "Well now Mister Bisset, what brings you to my bridge?" said Will in the same level tone. "I'm the replacement junior Third Officer, sir". "Are you indeed?" replied Will, "well there's a thing. In that case Mister Bisset, I suggest you report to Staff Captain Anderson at once. He's short-handed." Without even asking where he could find Anderson, Bestic saluted and replied, "Yes sir." As he turned to leave the bridge he thought fleetingly of telling the Captain that his name wasn't Bisset, but he decided against it. He already felt that Captain Turner was the sort of Captain that you certainly could not take liberties with, but rather tended to place absolute faith in. So what did it matter if he didn't get your name right?

In fact, Will had got his name right. It was just a quirk of his to deliberately mispronounce the surname of any new and unproven junior officer. If the officer made the grade, he'd know, when the Captain suddenly called him by his correct name.

Will had in fact formed a favourable first impression of "Bisset." The uniform had actually clinched it, as it showed that this officer was not afraid of hard work and obviously had not formed too high an opinion of his own importance. Had the uniform been downright shabby or obviously uncleaned, Will would have probably had him escorted off the ship, but it had just the right degree of practicality about it to please his eye. Not that he showed it, of course. But as Will suspected, Bestic was in fact only just out of sailing ships and hadn't had time to suffer from delusions of the grandeur of officer status. Time would tell if "Bisset" was made of the right material, but somehow Will thought that he was.

Luchow's restaurant 110 E 14th St. New York.
Circa 1915

70

Homeward bound-Destiny beckons...

At Pier 54 in New York harbour at 08:00 on the morning of Saturday 1st May, the *Lusitania* began embarkation. At the head of the gangway stood the ship's Purser, the Chief Steward and some of his staff ready to receive the passengers. With a Master-at-Arms on each side of the gangway, it must have looked like an official reception committee, except that the Captain wasn't present.

Will Turner was up on the bridge. Archie Bryce had reported the engineers' section ready for sea. All available boilers were on line, steam pressure was up and smoke gently furled from *Lusitania's* funnels, all of which were now painted black under Admiralty instructions, as opposed to Cunard red. Will walked out onto the bridge wing and looked down at the dockside. There was a bevy of reporters and a newsreel team on the pier. Will took his pipe out of his right hand pocket, and filled its black sandblasted briar bowl with his favourite dark tobacco. He tamped it down and lit it, puffing contentedly. Even now, he mused, she still makes the news when she sails.

As the black briar pipe warmed in his hand, Will noticed the figure of Charles Sumner, the Cunard Superintendent, making a beeline for the news reporters, one of whom was brandishing a newspaper. Well, whatever it was, he thought, Sumner could handle it.

At 08.30 hours, somewhat later than usual as the ship's scheduled departure had been delayed whilst passengers and cargo from another ship were transferred to the *Lusitania*, Will went to his day cabin for breakfast. The meal never varied. Aboard ship or at home, breakfast was two grilled kippers, two boiled eggs and thick scones heavily buttered and spread with orange marmalade, accompanied by a pot of tea, and when in New York, the *New York Tribune* newspaper.

Duly breakfasted, Will leafed through the Tribune. He almost didn't notice it at first but right next to Cunard's advertisement for *Lusitania's* departure was a black-bordered announcement boldly headed, "NOTICE." It read as follows:

> *"Travellers intending to embark on the Atlantic voyage are reminded that a state of war exists between Germany and her allies and Great Britain and her allies; that the zone of war includes the waters adjacent to the British Isles; that, in accordance with formal notice given by the Imperial German Government, vessels flying the flag of Great Britain, or any of her allies, are liable to destruction in those waters and that travellers sailing in the war zone on ships of Great Britain or her allies do so at their own risk."*
>
> IMPERIAL GERMAN EMBASSY. WASHINGTON D.C.

Was this a direct threat to his ship?! Will decided to seek out Sumner. By 10:20 hours, mysterious telegrams began to arrive in the ship's Marconi room. The telegrams were addressed to prominent passengers and warned against sailing on the *Lusitania*. The ship's Marconi operator held them back and checked with Will and Sumner, who retained them, realising that these telegrams were originated by a newspaper. Sumner then had Pier 54 cleared of reporters with the exception of the newsreel team and two members of the Press Association. There were no more telegrams.

At 11:00 hours, Archie Bryce came to the bridge to see Will. He was beginning to be concerned about the steam pressure. It wasn't critical yet, but if they didn't sail soon, he would have to release some of the pressure, which would mean another delay while it was raised again in order to sail.

Will had still not received his Admiralty sailing instructions at 11:15hours. Usually, one of Sir Courtenay Bennett's staff brought them to the ship. Sir Courtenay fulfiled the role of Senior Naval Officer for New York. His office was amongst those of Cunard and they had telephoned a message for Will to come at once. Donning his bowler, Will made his way to Sir Courtenay's office. On his way, he

72

stopped off at Sumner's office to check on alternative passenger accommodation on other ships. Will was fully expecting the *Lusitania's* departure to be cancelled or seriously delayed due to the German warnings.

An air of apprehension prevailed amongst the passengers aboard the *Lusitania*; would she sail? Passengers eyed one another, seeing whom, if anyone would suddenly decide to disembark. Where was the Captain?

At that moment, Will was just leaving Sir Courtenay Bennett's office. No specific sailing instructions had arrived for him so Sir Courtenay told him to adopt the same course and instructions as he had used for his last return trip. He was therefore to maintain wireless telegraphy silence, except in cases of a due emergency. After clearing Fastnet by at least 12 miles, he was to maintain a minimum distance of ten miles between his ship and the South coast of Ireland. He was given wireless related instructions, the current Naval code and told to use the No.1 edition of the merchant code for transmission, if necessary. He was also handed the details of his Naval escort, the cruiser HMS *Juno*, whom he was to meet ten miles South and not more than 40 miles to the West of Fastnet. Lastly he was handed the British embassy's despatch bag, which was to be thrown overboard if the ship was attacked. Its lead weights would carry it to the bottom. As an afterthought, Sir Courtenay informed him that an American ship had just been attacked by a German U-boat in the Irish Sea.

As Will arrived back at the *Lusitania*, he found that the press, having sensed the mood of the passengers, were badgering some of the more prominent ones for some kind of reaction or quote. They had singled out Alfred Vanderbilt, the millionaire and Charles Frohman, the famous theatre producer. Will walked straight into the little throng and turned to face the reporters. He told them to come back in ten minutes and they would hold a small press conference on the main deck. This gave Vanderbilt and Frohman a chance to recover from the badgering and compose themselves. Ten minutes later, Vanderbilt and Frohman appeared on either side of Commodore Turner and jocularly answered the reporters' questions. The newsreel team was also present.

During the ten minute interview, Will, Frohman and Vanderbilt made light of the German warning, emphasised the *Lusitania's* speed and the fact that she was a civilian passenger liner. The interview swiftly over, Will went straight to the bridge and rang "Stand by" on the main engine telegraphs. Archie Bryce breathed a great sigh of relief as he rang the repeater from the engine room.

Shortly after noon, the gangways were landed and the ropes securing her to Pier 54 were cast off. The band played on the quarterdeck and the *Lusitania*, bedecked with flags, was nudged away from the pier by three harbour tugs. As her bow was pointed downstream, the docks reverberated to the stentorian blast of her whistle. The tugs cast off in midstream and *Lusitania's* turbines began to churn the Hudson River into foam. *Lusitania* was going home.

Lusitania's last departure from New York

74

View from Lusitania's port side boat deck, leaving New York

With the statue of Liberty sliding astern, *Lusitania* had one brief stop to make before heading out into the Atlantic. Three miles out, at the limit of U.S. territorial waters, was a small blockading force of Royal Navy cruisers, one of which was a former passenger liner now fulfiling the role of armed merchant cruiser. Will recognised her immediately, even though she was now HMS *Caronia*.

The reason for the brief stop was to drop off a camera and a short report Will had penned as the ship left New York. Shortly after the tugs had cast off, the Master-at-Arms had discovered three unauthorised persons near a pantry. It did not take the Master-at-Arms long to ascertain that the three men were Germans. Having locked the men in the pantry and confiscated the camera, the Master-at-Arms reported it to Staff Captain Anderson, who in turn reported it to Will. It seems likely that the three men were trying to obtain photographic evidence that the *Lusitania* was armed. One of the Admiralty installed gun mountings was close to the location where they were discovered. Will was taking no chances. The camera, plates and his report would be handed to *Caronia* and the three Germans would be given free passage to England in the most comfortable cells on the Atlantic.

As the *Lusitania* neared the *Caronia*, a rowing boat came over to collect the items and to give *Lusitania* the *Caronia*'s crew letters to take back to England. Will went briefly out onto the port bridge wing to wave to his former shipmates on board *Caronia*.

As *Caronia*'s party departed, *Lusitania* hauled down all her flags and set out across the Atlantic for home. Her destiny awaited her.

War Zone...

The early evening of Thursday, May 6th, 1915 found Will Turner in his usual position on the port side of the bridge. His mood could best be described as pensive. So far, the voyage had been uneventful and the previous day he'd even found time to tie a complicated knot from his days in sail. Having completed a four stranded Turk's head; he'd decided to send it, via his messenger, to the officer's wardroom with his compliments and a request for an identical one to be returned to him forthwith.

The ship's Chief Officer, Mr. Piper, had taken the Captain's handiwork with more than a feeling of irritation and explained to the officers that "the old man" had only done it because he thought they couldn't. The task of replicating the knot fell to Bestic as he was not long out of sail and was also the only one in the wardroom who could identify the knot in the first place. It had amused Will to discover that it was the new junior Third Officer rather than the Chief Officer, or First Officer Jones who'd accomplished the task.

But a Marconi message delivered to him whilst he was at a small party in Charles Frohman's suite had brought him back to the bridge. The short message was doubly disturbing due to its incompleteness. It simply read; "*SUBMARINES ACTIVE OFF THE SOUTH COAST OF IRELAND*" Will asked for a repeat in case some of the message had been lost in transmission. The reply was identical. Perhaps when they met *Juno* in the morning, she might have some definite instructions for him. In the meantime, Will gave orders for the lifeboats to be swung out and made ready and for all watertight doors to be closed except those which were necessary to keep open for the working of the ship. The lookouts were doubled and all bright lights extinguished. The *Lusitania* forged ahead at just over 20 knots, which with one boiler room shut down, was close to her maximum speed.

At present, there was nothing more he could do. He decided

to go down to the first class dining room for dinner. This was the one mealtime he would have to spend with his passengers, and custom decreed that he should attend the concert in the first class smoking room afterwards. More importantly, he would also have to address the passengers after the concert.

The concert over, a small lectern was placed at one end of the first class smoking room and Will took his place behind it. He decided to dispense with the customary speech and simply hold a question and answer session. He felt that this would be more informative for the passengers and would also save time for him. He was anxious to return to the bridge.

The passengers had noted that the lifeboats were swung out and ready. This concerned them more than the daily boat drills had. The boat drills did not involve any passengers having to get into a lifeboat, only crew. Some passengers found it mildly amusing to watch an officer blow his whistle whilst six crewmen got into the boat and then got out of it again. Much has subsequently been made of Captain Turner's "failure" to conduct proper boat drills during the *Lusitania's* final voyage. What exactly would have been considered a proper drill has never actually been stated. To swing out and fill the boats with passengers, then lower them over the side with the ship making 20 knots on the high seas, is patently a dangerous practice. To have stopped the ship then practiced abandoning her, would have presented a sitting target to any German U-boat that may have been in the area. To load the boats with passengers and then unload them again would have been pointless. To swing them out and then have empty lifeboats, each weighing five tons, dangling over the side whilst the crew practiced lowering them with the ship making 20 knots, is also clearly absurd and would probably only have resulted in damage. The daily boat drills, farcical though they may seem to us at this remove, were merely for the visual reassurance of the passengers. They served no useful purpose to the crew, but Will could obviously not tell the passengers this fact.

Will explained to the assembled passengers that in the early hours of the next morning they would be entering the so-called war zone. Therefore he had duly ordered a slight reduction in the *Lusitania's* speed, from 20 knots to 18 knots. Will went to great lengths to reassure the passengers that these were merely routine precautions and he closed the session with a further assurance that upon entering the war zone, a Royal Navy cruiser would be alongside to escort them to Liverpool. "Tomorrow" he told them, "we shall be securely in the hands of the Royal Navy".

Will took his leave of the passengers and went straight to the bridge. He arrived just in time to receive another Admiralty message. It read:

"TO ALL BRITISH SHIPS 0005:

TAKE LIVERPOOL PILOT AT BAR AND AVOID HEADLANDS. PASS HARBOURS AT FULL SPEED. STEER MID-CHANNEL COURSE. SUBMARINES OFF FASTNET."
Those last three last words worried him. How far off Fastnet?

Will told the Marconi room to acknowledge the signal. He then gave orders to the now doubled lookouts to be especially vigilant and to report anything suspicious, however slight, immediately. Stewards were also reminded to ensure that portholes were securely closed and blacked out and to see that there were no gentlemen smoking cigars out on deck. Having done this, he went to his day cabin to consider his options.

Will sat at his desk and lit up his black pipe. Out of habit, he picked up his sextant, which had been with him since his days in sail. He used it first thing every morning to take an altitude of the sun. It comforted him and helped him to think. Now he needed to make two plans. A main plan and a bad weather plan. The area he was sailing into was notorious for fog and the barometer reading at that moment was giving every indication that he could expect some. He'd crossed the Atlantic on dead reckoning, as always, but he would need a sighting of some prominent feature on land at some point tomorrow in order to get a precise fix on his position.

He was in possession of his Admiralty sailing instructions from

Sir Courtenay Bennett. Those were fixed and he was not permitted to deviate from them unless they were countermanded by specific instructions from either a Royal Navy warship or a Marconi message from the Admiralty, and the latter was unlikely, due to the Admiralty's fear of the Germans intercepting the message. As things stood at the moment, his orders were to clear Fastnet by at least 12 miles, then maintain a minimum of ten miles between his ship and the South Coast of Ireland. One option of course was to divert up the West Coast of Ireland then come into Liverpool via the North Channel. He would thereby avoid Fastnet altogether and the submarines which the Admiralty now said were lurking there. Well, perhaps *Juno* would order him to do that at their rendezvous. But at the moment, he had to work on the basis of what he knew. First and foremost he decided because of that disturbing Marconi message, to clear Fastnet rock, which was an important landfall, by at least 20 miles. He'd reduced speed to 18 knots so as to pass Fastnet during near darkness. Will reasoned that if a U-boat was lurking anywhere near there, *Lusitania* would be much further out to sea than perhaps the U-boat Captain expected and by extinguishing all bright lights she would be harder to see and harder to identify.

He then studied the Admiralty advices to mariners. Possibly there would be something in there which could be of help? Some of them, it transpired, were of no use at all to man or beast. One said not to steer too far out whilst another warned not to come too close inshore. As neither recommended any specific distances, where did the safest course lie? He discarded those. There was one dated February 10th, 1915, which read:

"Vessels navigating in submarine areas should have their boats turned out and fully provisioned. The danger is greatest in the vicinity of ports and off prominent headlands on the coast. Important landfalls in this area should be made after dark whenever possible. So far as is consistent with particular trades and state of tides, vessels should make their ports at dawn."

That seemed like sound advice to Will. Another of the advices warned vessels to keep off the usual peacetime trade routes. That struck Will as sound advice too, though in his case it did not matter as his route was set by the Admiralty. In any case, the *Lusitania's* peacetime route was only three miles offshore. Tomorrow's route was to be at least ten miles offshore, if not further.

Another memo, also dated February 10th, 1915 recommended steering a serpentine course and making full speed if a U-boat was sighted. In Will's judgement, these advices made the most sense given his situation. He put all these to one side and filed the others away.

Turning to his tide tables and his chart, he noted that the best time to arrive in Liverpool was 04:00 hours on Saturday morning with the flood tide. There would be sufficient water over the bar and it would also be in accordance with making his port at dawn. He was cleared to proceed into Liverpool without a pilot, which would save him keeping *Lusitania* outside the bar and presenting a sitting target to any U-boat waiting outside port.

Timing his arrival thus, he simply worked backwards from Liverpool to plot his course and speed. In this way, the main plan could be easily modified to suit any adverse weather conditions which may be encountered. This done, Will left instructions to be called if anything materialised and then he turned in. He would have to be up very early as he anticipated meeting *Juno* shortly after dawn.

Will did not get much sleep that Thursday night. He was awakened six times with messages from the Marconi room. Each time it was the same message, a repeat of the earlier signal to all British ships. On the sixth instance, Will noted that it was a half hour to dawn so he sent his steward to fetch him some tea while he washed, shaved and dressed. Fateful Friday had begun.

Fateful Friday and Beyond...

As Will got up, he instinctively looked out of the window. He could see absolutely nothing. Fog had closed in around the *Lusitania*. Gulping down the last of the piping hot tea his steward had brought him; he went straight to the bridge.

The fog could be a godsend Will thought. Visibility was down to about 30 yards and he could only just discern the figures of the two lookouts on the bow. He doubted the chances of success for a U-boat in this weather. But the other problem was that he had also to meet *Juno* in this weather.

As soon as he'd reached the bridge, he ordered a further reduction in *Lusitania's* speed, to 15 knots. This was because of the fog. He had no wish to collide with HMS *Juno*, nor did he want to miss meeting her. He also checked that all watertight doors were still closed.

Though he did not like to disturb the passengers this early in the morning, there was one more thing he had to do. He gave orders for the ship's foghorn to be sounded, a call for *Juno* to hear, as well as an anti collision measure.

Next he went into the chart room. He didn't know exactly their position, but as near as he could figure it by dead reckoning, they were about 70 miles off Cape Clear. Beside the chart on the large table were the Admiralty advices which he'd selected the night before. He read them again now, because he thought it increasingly likely that he'd miss *Juno* in the fog.

Working on that basis, he still needed a mean speed of 18 knots to arrive at Liverpool at 04:00 next morning. He did not want to arrive there any earlier, but he would have some time in hand should the fog continue. He went back to the bridge and occupied the port side corner, as he always did when he was concerned. He was watching for *Juno*. As was usual when the captain was on the bridge, nobody spoke. Silence reigned supreme. *Lusitania* glided through the swirling fog at a steady 15 knots on course South 87 East, her foghorn booming out at regular intervals. Will could do nothing more at the moment. At 07:30 hours, he went down to his day cabin to breakfast.

He was about halfway through his kippers when there was a knock on his door. He disliked being disturbed whilst he was eating but his annoyance vanished when Archie Bryce entered the room. He motioned Archie to sit down at the breakfast table and invited him to pour himself a cup of tea. He'd wanted a word with Archie in any case. Will quickly outlined the situation to Archie. He told him of his overall plan to maintain the maximum cruising speed of 18 knots so as to arrive in Liverpool at 04:00 hours, but he wanted Archie to keep the steam pressure high just in case he rang down for the full speed of 21 knots in an emergency. Archie expressed mild alarm and asked Will if he thought the Germans might try to torpedo them. Will told him that he doubted it personally. Still, it was best not to take chances. Breakfast over, Archie went back to the engine room and Will went back up to the bridge. The foghorn boomed out its monotonous call and Will peered forward from the port side corner of his bridge. But where was HMS *Juno*?

Meanwhile, events and circumstances in London, Queenstown and on the Atlantic Ocean were beginning to assume a shape and form that would ultimately have a bearing on Will's life beyond his belief.

Admiralty House, Whitehall, London.

It had been a busy close to the week at the Admiralty. First Lord, Winston Churchill had left for France on Wednesday May 5th. Before he left, a briefing had taken place in the map room so that First Sea Lord Jacky Fisher and Admiral Oliver, who would deputise for Churchill in his absence, would be up to date with what was known as "the plot."

The plot referred to the great map of the world's Oceans on which was plotted the latest positions of German U-boats, (obtained by wireless intercepts, sighting reports, reports of sinkings, etc.) of units of the Royal Navy and any other important ships, such as those under Admiralty charter or others carrying important war supplies. The positions of each of the vessels on the plot was marked with a brightly coloured pin, colour coded to represent the type of vessel. On the head of each pin, to the scale of the map, was a disc, which represented the field of vision of a lookout on board that vessel. The plot was updated continually, as each piece of fresh information, once verified, came in. It was upon the plot that all operational decisions of the Admiralty were made.

The plot that Wednesday morning showed two U-boats on or near the Western approaches. *U-30* was shown North of Ireland and heading North Eastwards for home and *U-20* North West of Fastnet, heading South. Also shown near Fastnet, slightly to the South West, was the cruiser HMS *Juno*. The largest disc of all represented the *Lusitania*, shown well West of Fastnet but approaching at 20 knots. It did not take a genius to work out that one passenger liner, one warship and one enemy submarine were all converging on the same spot: Fastnet.

The decision was therefore taken to recall HMS *Juno* to Queenstown immediately, due to her vulnerability to submarine attack. She was of the *Eclipse* class built in 1898 and was now showing her age. Despite this, she was the flagship of cruiser force E based at Queenstown. Her construction was similar to the cruisers *Aboukir*, *Hogue* and *Cressy*, which had been sunk in September of 1914. One after the other, the cruisers were attacked by just one U-boat, one of Germany's older, paraffin-engined types, the U-9, commanded by Otto Weddigen. The cruisers had all capsized and sank went down rapidly with appalling loss of life, in the North Sea, in September 1914. It had become known as the "livebait squadron debacle." Those in charge at the Admiralty that Wednesday morning had no desire for a repeat of the incident. The very real danger to both ships was there for all to see, but only half of it, the danger to HMS *Juno*, was evidently realised.

Unfortunately, it would seem that the minds of Churchill and Fisher were obviously elsewhere during the briefing. Churchill was off to France that afternoon to take part in a Naval convention, the conclusion of which would bring Italy into the war on the side of the Allies. Then, as a diversion from the stresses and strains of his disastrous Dardanelles campaign, Churchill was off to see Sir John French make his attack on the Aubers ridge. Both the Prime Minister and Churchill's wife remonstrated with him not to stay in France beyond the conclusion of the Naval convention, which was merely a formality. Fisher argued with him about it too, but Churchill defied them all. He'd had enough of the Admiralty. It was a political cul-de-sac and his association with the Dardanelles campaign would not do him any good at all. He was looking for a way out and Sir John French might just provide it for him. If he courted favour with Sir John, he might be able to transfer from the Admiralty to a military position. He was looking forward to the trip.

Fisher's mind was pre-occupied with resentment. There was Churchill off to France on a "jolly" whilst he was left holding the fort, at such a critical time too. It was unforgivable as far as Fisher was concerned. Why should it all be left to him?

Admiral Oliver was tired of all the in fighting too. Fisher and Churchill differed on so many things recently that it was hard to know exactly what was happening. Now Churchill was off to France for five days and already Fisher looked like sliding into one of his sulks. Where would it all end?

The briefing ended with *Juno*'s immediate recall. She would be ordered to head South East during the night and then clear Fastnet by 50 miles. She was then to make for Queenstown with all speed.

No message was sent to Captain Turner of the *Lusitania* to advise him that his escort had been withdrawn. Nor was he informed of the now perilous situation he faced, in case such a sensitive piece of information was intercepted by the Germans. Churchill then hurried to Waterloo station to catch his train. Fisher went to lunch and then adjourned his activities for his afternoon sleep. Oliver returned to his office and dutifully carried on with his paperwork, in which he was habitually 24 hours behind.

Late that afternoon *U-20* sank a small schooner off Kinsale. The *Earl of Lathom* wasn't worth a torpedo. Her crew were allowed to abandon ship and then *U-20* sunk her by placing bombs aboard. A message reached the Admiralty, via Queenstown, around 21:30 hours that night. No action was taken other than to update the plot with *U-20*'s newest known position. By midnight, news had come in that the British steamer *Cayo Romano* had been attacked off Queenstown. Fortunately, *U-20*'s torpedo had missed its target. Once more, *U-20*'s coloured pin was moved further eastward on the Admiralty's map. This time, action was taken. The signal *"SUBMARINES ACTIVE OFF SOUTH COAST OF IRELAND"* was broadcast, albeit 20 hours after the event. Given that the Admiralty knew to within a few hours the position of *U-20*, it seems rather a halfhearted measure to have taken.

On the next day, Thursday May 6th, *U-20* was in the vicinity of the Conningbeg lightship. This lightship marks the entrance to St. George's Channel and the last leg of the voyage to Liverpool. In a position approximately 12 miles East of the lightship, *U-20* chased and sank the Harrison line steamer *Candidate*. She was torpedoed and sunk by gunfire. Later that day, *Candidate's* sister ship, *Centurion* suffered the same sort of fate in roughly the same area. *U-20* also attacked, though without success, the White Star liner *Arabic*. News of the *Candidate's* sinking reached the Admiralty by 11:00 hours on May 6th, but they in turn did not inform Queenstown till 24 hours later. By 03:40 hours on the morning of Friday, May 7th, the Admiralty also knew the fate of the *Centurion*.

Queenstown

The man in charge at Queenstown was Vice Admiral Sir Charles Henry Coke. He was responsible for the defence of area 21 which extended from Fastnet rock to Carnsore point. His force was derisively known as the "Gilbert and Sullivan navy." He had a motley collection of ageing torpedo boats, an armed yacht, some fishing boats and a motorboat with which to protect the 285 miles of Ireland's South

86

coast. The armed yacht had only one gun and the fastest vessel in his "Navy" was capable of 11 knots.

Also based at Queenstown under Rear Admiral Sir Horace Hood was cruiser Squadron E. This force consisted of five ageing cruisers of which HMS *Juno*, an *Eclipse* class cruiser of 1898 vintage, mounting 11 guns of six inch calibre, was the flagship and on a good day she was capable of 16 and a half knots.

This force was charged with the defence and patrol responsibilities of the entire Western approaches; that is to say, the point where all the major shipping lanes converged; Britain's lifeline to the rest of the world. Though totally inadequate for their assigned task, these ships were the best available to Coke at the time. HMS *Juno* was simply the best of a bad bunch, but something was better than nothing.

Vice Admiral Coke had by nature, something of a nervous disposition. He worried greatly about his responsibilities given the woefully inadequate state of his forces. But operationally, his hands were just as much tied as Will Turner's were. The Admiralty laid down strict instructions which must be adhered to at all times unless directly countermanded by the appropriate authority. Among those instructions was one that stated that all Marconi messages should be of a general and negative nature. Ships were not to be told to go to specific areas or given any specific course as the Germans might intercept the message and then head straight for that area.

By the morning of Friday, May 7th, Coke must have been pacing his office sick with worry. He knew there was a U-boat off Queenstown. He knew about other attacks and the sinkings off Kinsale and the Conningbeg Lightship. He knew that the *Lusitania* was due and he also knew that her escort, HMS *Juno*, had been withdrawn.

The Admiralty had ordered him to protect the *Lusitania* in the best way that he was able. But how could he protect her without telling her where the danger was? It was absurd. *"SUBMARINES ACTIVE OFF THE SOUTH COAST OF IRELAND"* was certainly general and negative in nature. It was the only thing he could think of. But he knew it was not enough.

87

Atlantic Ocean, 25 miles South of Cape Clear, 10:30 hours

The fog still swirled around the *Lusitania*. Will was still very concerned that he would not find *Juno* if it persisted. On the other hand, he still doubted that any U-boat would find *Lusitania* in it, so if it did persist it would provide him with near perfect cover. But he must establish his position before he even dared to approach St. George's Channel. The entrance to the channel was 24 miles wide with rocks and shoals on either side. There would also be other shipping using the channel. He could not set an accurate course without a fix.

At 11:00 hours, the *Lusitania* broke through the fog into hazy sunshine. To port was an indistinct smudge, which was the Irish coastline. But there was no sign of any other ships. No *Juno*.

Will immediately ordered an increase in speed, back to 18 knots. The foghorn ceased its booming call.

Barely had he done this when a messenger from the Marconi room brought him a signal. It was 12 words, but Will did not recognise the cypher. It was from Vice Admiral Coke in Queenstown, relayed through the naval wireless station at Valentia. Because of the high-grade code used to send the signal, Will would have to take it down to his day cabin to work on it.

At 11:55 hours there was a knock on Will's door. It was the messenger with another signal from the Admiralty; Will broke off from his decoding work to read it. It said: *"SUBMARINE ACTIVE IN SOUTHERN PART OF IRISH CHANNEL, LAST HEARD OF TWENTY MILES SOUTH OF CONNINGBEG LIGHT VESSEL. MAKE CERTAIN LUSITANIA GETS THIS."*

This gave Will another problem. According to this latest message, another U-boat was operating in the very middle of the channel he was aiming for. If this were true, then despite his Admiralty instructions, a mid channel course was now out of the question. True, *Lusitania* wouldn't arrive there till later and it would be dark when she did, but it did not make sense to Will to drive his ship toward a submarine he now knew to be there. More than ever, he now had to determine his exact position, if he was going to have to play a potentially deadly game of cat and mouse with a U-boat in a narrow channel entrance. But first he decided to finish deciphering Coke's earlier message. Perhaps it might contain something concrete upon which he could make a plan.

By 12:10 hours he had finished decoding it completely. What he read galvanised him. He went straight to the bridge. HMS *Juno* didn't matter any more, in fact unbeknown to him; she was now docking in Queenstown having been urgently recalled.

Immediately he entered the bridge he altered the ships course 20 degrees to port. Third Officer Lewis was then dispatched to make a fast round of the ship to check that all ports on the lower decks were closed. The turn to port was so sudden that many passengers momentarily lost their balance. The *Lusitania* was now closing to the land at 18 knots on course North 67 East. Will needed to fix his position immediately. The clock on the bridge said 12:15 hours, GMT.

Atlantic Ocean, 22 miles off Waterford

The German submarine *U-20* blew her tanks and surfaced. The fog, which had been troubling her commander, Kapitan-Leutnant Walther Schwieger, had finally cleared. In many ways, it had been a disappointing patrol but thankfully, it was nearly over. The successes of the last two days had improved the morale of the crew. But they were now down to the last three torpedoes and his orders were to save two for the trip home, just in case they encountered an enemy warship and had to fight their way out of it.

At just after 12:00 hours GMT while they had been submerged, the sound of very powerful propellers had been heard passing over them. Coming up to periscope depth, Schwieger saw a cruiser rapidly disappearing toward Queenstown. It was no use trying to catch it. The cruiser was making all speed and was zig-zagging. "Damn!" he'd thought, "a prime target and we've missed it!"

Schwieger checked his watch. It was 12:20 hoursGMT as the *U-20* headed back toward Fastnet at full speed.

Kapitan Leutnant Walther Schwieger: Commander of U 20

At 12:40 hours, whilst *Lusitania* was still on course N 67 E, Will received another Admiralty signal. This one read: *"SUBMARINE FIVE MILES SOUTH OF CAPE CLEAR, PROCEEDING WEST WHEN SIGHTED AT 10.00 AM."* He allowed himself a slight smile. This latest signal meant that the immediate danger was passed. He had been right; the fog undoubtedly saved them. The submarine off Fastnet

90

U 20 sights Lusitania

had now evidently given up. Cape Clear was many miles astern of *Lusitania*. The entrance to St. George's Channel and therefore the next U-boat threat was still four to five hours away. For now, he was safely in the middle. Yet the most curious thing in all this was that there was no submarine off Cape Clear. There never had been, The "Fastnet" submarine was obviously a figment of someone's imagination. But the "Conningbeg" submarine was real enough. Only now of course, it was no longer near Conningbeg.

At 13:20 hours GMT, *U-20* was still running on the surface, heading back toward Fastnet. Schwieger was up on the conning tower with the lookouts, the air was considerably fresher up there. Suddenly, the starboard lookout saw smoke off the *U-20*'s starboard bow.

Schwieger focussed his binoculars on it. One, two, three, four funnels. Only the biggest ships had four. He estimated the distance between them to be 12 to 14 miles. It would be a long shot, but if the

91

ship was heading for Queenstown, it might just be possible. As the diving klaxon screeched out it's warning, *U-20* altered course to intercept the ship, submerging as she did so.

At 13:40 hours GMT, Will saw a landmark as familiar to him as his own front door. A Long promontory with a lighthouse on top of it, which was painted with black and white horizontal bands. The Old head of Kinsale. For centuries, the Old Head of Kinsale had been an important landmark for the world's mariners. It was, in a way, like the *Lusitania* herself; impossible to mistake. Now that he knew where he was he ordered *Lusitania's* course reverted to South 87 East, steady. Turning back to his officers on the bridge, Will noticed "Bisset", due to go off watch in about 15 minutes. "Ah, Bisset. Do you know how to take a four point bearing?" he asked. Bestic certainly did. He also knew that it took the best part of an hour with the ship's course and speed having to remain rock steady whilst it was done. "Yes sir," he replied. "Good. Then kindly take one off that lighthouse, will you?" And with that Will left the bridge and went into the chartroom. He knew what "Bisset" was thinking, but attention to detail was one of the things that would one day make a good junior officer into a good master.

Bestic needn't have worried. Lewis came back at 14:00 hours and relieved him anyway, knowing what the "old man" had done. Bestic took the first set of bearing figures to Will in the chartroom on his way off the bridge. Bestic then went down to his small cabin to finish writing up the ship's log.

Using the figures that Bestic had given him, Will worked out that they were now 14 miles offshore and slightly West of the Old Head. He needed the full set of bearing figures to be exact, but it was a good start. He now had to plot a safe course through the mine free channel into Queenstown harbour. They were not going to Liverpool after all, not yet anyway. The message from Vice Admiral Coke, which was sent in the high-grade naval code, was ordering him to divert *Lusitania* into Queenstown immediately. Exactly as had previously happened when he'd brought the *Transylvania* over with that big gun lashed to the foredeck. Standard Admiralty practice in situations of grave peril. Obviously, Will thought, they were not going to allow him to take his ship into the narrow entrance of St. George's channel knowing that there was a U-boat waiting for him.

But what Will didn't know, because the Admiralty hadn't told him, was that the "U-boat off Conningbeg Lightship" report was already 28 hours old. They hadn't told him that it had sunk two cargo ships there, attacked a large passenger liner and had in fact sunk a sailing ship off Queenstown two days ago. Nor did they tell him that since he left New York, no fewer than 23 merchant ships had been attacked by German U-boats in the waters around Britain and that almost all of them had been sunk. The other thing they didn't tell him was that they were certain that this U-boat was now on it's way home and at that moment, was off Queenstown, somewhere. Though they had specifically informed Rear Admiral Hood aboard the *Juno* of this at 07:45 hours that morning.

Kapitan-Leutnant Walther Schwieger studied the big ship through *U-20*'s attack periscope. Calling to the U-boat's pilot, Schwieger said, "Four funnels, schooner rig, upwards of 20,000 tons and making about 22 knots." Lanz, the pilot, checked in his copies of Jane's fighting ships and Brassey's naval annual. They were two standard British publications and every German U-boat carried them to identify potential targets. Lanz called back to Schwieger "Either the *Lusitania* or the *Mauretania*. Both listed as armed merchant cruisers and used for trooping." *U-20* prepared for action. One G type torpedo was loaded into a forward tube. Wiesbach, the torpedo officer reported the tube ready for firing. As he did, Schwieger noticed the target altering course. He could not believe his luck! He noted later in his logbook "The ship turns to starboard then takes a course to Queenstown....." Exactly what he had hoped she would do!

At a range of 550 yards, Schwieger gave the deadly order, "Fire One!" The torpedo cleared the tube and streaked towards it's target at 38 knots, it's running depth set at three metres, about ten feet.

Will Turner had come out of the chartroom and was standing

in his usual place on the port side of the bridge. He was watching Third Officer Lewis working on the four-point bearing. Beyond him, stood a Quartermaster right out on the bridge wing acting as a lookout. There was another on the starboard bridge wing. But it was from the crow's nest that the sudden warning came, via the telephone. "Torpedo coming on the starboard side!"

Will looked to starboard in shocked disbelief just in time to see the white streak of water. But before he could even shout a helm order, the torpedo struck the ship with a sound, which he later recalled, was "like a heavy door being slammed shut." Almost instantaneously came a second, much larger explosion, which physically rocked the ship. A tall column of water and debris shot skyward.

Lusitania is struck by the torpedo

At this moment, Junior Third Officer Bestic was in his cabin. The baggage master had sent a messenger with a request that he come forthwith to the baggage room to oversee the unloading of the passengers' luggage. Now that they were making an unscheduled stop at Queenstown, the baggage master thought it prudent to start piling some of the luggage on the foredeck, in order to save time, and possibly passenger complaints, when the ship docked. Bestic was just about to follow the messenger down to the forward hold when he realised that he was still wearing his best uniform. Pausing to change into that working uniform of his ultimately saved his life, as there were no survivors from the baggage room. They were all killed when the torpedo struck the ship just below the area where they were working.

Up on the bridge, Will quickly looked at the ship's indicator board. It was going absolutely mad, showing extensive fire and flooding in the whole of the forward section. The column of water and debris now cascaded down and wrecked one of the forward starboard lifeboats. A glance at the commutator revealed that the *Lusitania* was already listing five degrees to starboard and was also down by the head. The clock on the bridge said 14:10 hours.

Watching events through his periscope, Schwieger could not believe that so much havoc could have been wrought by one torpedo. He noted in his log that "an unusually heavy detonation" had taken place and noted that a second explosion had also occurred which he put down to "boilers, coal or powder." He also noticed that the torpedo had hit the *Lusitania* further forward of where he had aimed it. He therefore revised his estimate of the *Lusitania's* speed to "not more than 20 knots." After allowing Lanz a quick look, Schwieger brought the periscope down and *U-20* headed back to sea.

On the bridge of the *Lusitania*, the slant of the deck grew steeper. Will shouted to Quartermaster Johnston, who was at the helm, to close any watertight doors that remained open and to put the helm over toward land. The bows of the liner were dipping toward the sea at an alarming rate. Looking forward, Will could see instantly that his ship was doomed. He gave the orders to abandon ship and also instructed Second Officer Hefford to send the ship's carpenter forward to assess the damage. Will then went out onto the port bridge wing and looked back along the boat deck.

The first thing he saw was that all the port side lifeboats had swung inboard, which meant that all those on the starboard side had swung outboard. The starboard ones could be launched, though with a little difficulty, but the port side boats would be virtually impossible to launch.

Each of the wooden lifeboats weighed five tons unladen. To steady them, each boat had a metal chain called a snubbing chain, which held it to the deck. Prior to lowering the boat, the release pin had to be knocked out using a hammer. Otherwise the boat would remain chained to the deck.

Looking forward again, Will also felt a breeze on his face. The ship was still under way. Beaching her was out of the question. He knew they were 14 miles from shore and she was sinking so fast that they'd never make it. He had to stop the ship so that the boats could be safely lowered. Instinctively, he rang down to the engine room for full speed astern. The engine room dutifully complied and the valves on the steam pipes to the low pressure turbines blew out, which also blew the end cap off of a condenser up on the boat deck that nearly took Third Officer Lewis' head off.

Realising the mistake, the engines were reverted to "full ahead" to relieve the pressure on the valves. Unfortunately, the overall steam pressure had now dropped drastically, having escaped through the blown valves, so now the *Lusitania's* massive turbines were virtually out of commission. There was hardly enough steam pressure left to drive them.

At 14.11, the *Lusitania* started sending distress signals from the Marconi room. "*SOS, SOS, SOS. COME AT ONCE. BIG LIST. 10 MILES SOUTH OLD KINSALE. MFA.*"

The last three letters were the *Lusitania's* call sign.

When Vice Admiral Coke received his copy of that distress

signal, it must have seemed to him as though his worst nightmare had come true. He had tried in vain all morning to obtain a firm decision from the Admiralty in London. However, Fisher had been "unavailable" all morning, Churchill was in France and Oliver it seemed, would do nothing off his own bat, or at least not without consulting Fisher, perhaps. In the end, Coke had been so worried by the obvious danger that he had taken it upon himself to divert the *Lusitania* into Queenstown. Unfortunately, it was all too late. Still, there was something he could do. He sent a signal to Rear Admiral Hood in *Juno* and sent him to the rescue. Hood cleared Queenstown in a remarkably short time and headed out toward the *Lusitania's* last known position. Coke then sent a detailed signal to the Admiralty, advising them of what had happened and of his actions and the measures he had taken.

On the *Lusitania*, the list indicator had just gone through the 15-degree mark. Will Turner was still out on the port side wing of the bridge. He had ordered Staff Captain Anderson not to lower any of the boats until the ship had lost a sufficient amount of her momentum to render it safe. In some cases, on the port side, that meant getting the passengers out of the lifeboats in order to lower them to the rail. But the passengers did not want to get out of the boats.

At boat station no.2, junior Third Officer Bestic was in charge. Standing on the after davit, he was trying to keep order and explain that due to the heavy list, the boat could not be lowered. Suddenly, he heard the sound of a hammer striking the linkpin to the snubbing chain. Before the word "NO!" left his lips, the chain was freed and the five-ton lifeboat laden with over 50 passengers, swung inboard and crushed those standing on the boat deck against the superstructure. Unable to take the strain, the men at the davits let go of the falls and boat two, plus the collapsible boat stowed behind it, slid down the deck towing a grisly collection of injured passengers and jammed under the bridge wing, right beneath the spot where Will Turner was.

Bestic, determined to stop the same situation arising at the next boat station, jumped along to no.4 boat, just as somebody

97

knocked out the linkpin. Bestic darted out of the way as no.4 boat slid down the deck maiming and killing countless more people, before crashing into the wreckage of the first two boats. Bestic then fought his way through the crowd to boat six where Anderson, seeing what had happened, was trying to get the people out of the lifeboat.

But as fast as some got out, others got in. Anderson sent Bestic back to the bridge with a request that the port side trim tanks were to be flooded to counteract the starboard list. They could then lower the port side boats. Having dispatched Bestic, Anderson gave orders for everyone to get out of the boats whilst the crew and some of the male passengers manhandled the boats over the rail. By the time Bestic came back to tell him that there was no power to the trimming system, the shout had gone round that Anderson was preventing women and children from entering the lifeboats. Driven by panic, passengers swarmed into lifeboats 6, 8 and 10. One after the other they careered down the deck to join lifeboats 2 and 4.

Lusitania sinking

Standing on the port bridge wing looking down on the carnage, Will was horrified by the spectacle. A shout from Quartermaster Johnston telling him that the list had increased to 20 degrees, cut through his horror. Turning away from the grisly scene he saw that the *Lusitania's* bows were now completely underwater.

Fresh screams from behind him told Will that another lifeboat had added to the carnage below him. The *Lusitania* was set to capsize completely unless her bows struck the bottom first. "Twenty five degrees to starboard!" Shouted Quartermaster Johnston. "Then save yourself" Will told him. Johnston needed no second telling. He hurriedly put on a lifebelt and simply stepped into the water, which was creeping inexorably up the starboard side of the bridge.

Will was now alone out on the port wing of the bridge. As the stern rose up out of the water, Will gripped the signal halyards and looked aft as the boat deck and *Lusitania's* four immense funnels towered over him. Just then, the ship's doctor strenuously worked his way 'uphill' to stand with him. Neither man spoke but it was the last Will saw of him.

Lusitania's forward momentum suddenly ceased. Looking quickly forward toward the liner's bows, Will realised that they'd struck the bottom. The sea was now swirling over the bridge floor. Will went back inside and worked his way into the chartroom. He seized the chart he'd been working on and quickly stuffed it inside his tunic, though he didn't know why. The *Lusitania's* stern now began to settle back and a surge of water flooded the bridge, sweeping Will out of the door and off the ship. As the *Lusitania* sank beneath the waves, that same surge of water swept junior Third Officer Bestic out through the first class entrance hall into the Ocean. The *Lusitania* was gone. It was 14:28 hours GMT.

Only six lifeboats out of a total of 48 were afloat amid the wreckage. As the survivors clung to hope in the water, some of them noticed a warship, which seemed to be heading directly for them. Their spirits lifted momentarily but then hope turned to despair as suddenly the warship turned around and then headed back to whence it came. It was another two hours before fishing boats out of Kinsale reached the scene of the disaster, though many in the water would never know.

Will Turner had found a chair to cling to. He was one of the first to be rescued by the steamer *Bluebell*. He was brought aboard after almost three hours in the water then wrapped in a hot blanket and given a mug of something hot to drink. He sat alone, huddled into a corner feeling an overpowering sense of loss.

Sometime later, the crew of the *Bluebell* fished Bestic out of the water. He was the first to actually recognise Will. Bestic sat down next to him and said, "I'm glad to see you made it, sir." Will looked at him and said coldly "Why should you be? You're not that fond of me." Bestic felt hurt by the remark but put it down to the ordeal they'd been through. "All the same sir, I'm glad to see you alive," he said. Then Bestic thought it best to just leave Will alone, so he moved off somewhere else.

As Bestic left, someone else recognised the lonely figure of Will Turner. She was a passenger whose young son had been drowned when one of the starboard lifeboats, hastily lowered, had hit the water bows first and smashed to pieces. She accused him of a lack of organisation and discipline among the crew of the *Lusitania*. She told him flatly that her son's death had been completely unnecessary. But her words seemed to wash over Will Turner, who never looked up from the drinking mug he held in his hands, his mind unable to come to terms with the enormity of what had happened.

When *Bluebell* docked in Queenstown, Will shuffled down the gangplank still wrapped in the blanket and looking for all to see, like an old shabby Indian from the wild West. There were subdued cheers from the townspeople on the quay, but Will never heard them as he was shepherded off to temporary accommodation in a hotel.

Meanwhile, the dead as well as the living were brought ashore. Even at that early stage, it was obvious to anyone watching that the former far outnumbered the latter.

Admiralty House, Whitehall, London.

When the news from Queenstown that the *Lusitania* had been sunk reached Admiral Oliver, he took it at once to Fisher, who was now available. Upon realising that Coke had sent HMS *Juno* out again, Fisher sent a signal recalling her at once. The *Lusitania* had been sunk by a U-boat. Fisher was not going to add a cruiser to the submarine's tally.

That done, Fisher and Oliver set about raising a smokescreen to cover Admiralty House. Given their previously inexplicable inactivity during the morning of that fateful Friday, the pair now worked feverishly into the night and over the weekend. Survival was undoubtedly their prime motive.

Admiral Oliver called the Director of the Trade Division, Captain Richard Webb, into his office urgently. After an intense discussion, the two issued a wealth of signals requesting information from various authorities in Queenstown, Liverpool, New York and London. Captain Webb then set about the task of compiling a special *Lusitania* memorandum, which was to form the basis of the Admiralty's view of the disaster. Captain Webb's memorandum was also to have a most profound effect upon Will Turner in due course. Admiral Oliver meanwhile, was busy collecting ALL signals which had been sent to, or received from, the *Lusitania* into one special file, to await Churchill's return from France.

Kinsale, Saturday May 8th, 1915.

The morning after the disaster brought a visitor to Will Turner. He was the Kinsale coroner, Mr. John Horgan and the purpose of his visit was to formally and personally serve a summons on Will, to appear at an inquest he was holding that afternoon at the Old Market House in Kinsale, into the deaths of the five persons whose bodies had been washed ashore within his district. Horgan would not release the five bodies until his official duty as coroner had been discharged. He then left to serve summonses on as many other survivors as he could.

At the Old Market House that afternoon, Horgan had assembled a jury of twelve local shopkeepers and fisherman. One after

101

the other, the survivors were called to testify as to what had taken place. Will Turner testified that one torpedo had struck the ship and that its explosion was followed by a massive internal explosion which rent the ship, and that the *Lusitania* had sunk in only 18 minutes. The inquest was then stopped at this point as the strain finally proved to be too much for Will. Having to relive the nightmare scenes of the sinking, the carnage on the port side boat deck and having spent nearly three hours in the water waiting for rescue, finally took its toll. Will bowed his head and burst into tears. As one observer at the proceedings later put it; "Captain Turner appeared at the inquest in a donated suit of badly fitting clothes and was obviously still suffering from the strain of his experiences. He looked, and was, a broken man."

Summing up, Horgan thanked Will for coming to the inquest and for being so helpful. He then directed the jury to return a verdict that the deceased had died as a result of prolonged immersion and exhaustion due to the sinking of the *Lusitania*, which in turn was caused by "torpedoes fired without warning from a German submarine." Horgan then charged the officers of the submarine, along with Kaiser Wilhelm and the German government with "wilful and wholesale murder." The final casualty figures were 1,201 men, women and children dead, out of a total of 1,962 persons on board. The official figures of 1,959 persons aboard and 1,198 dead, obviously do not include the three Germans who were locked in the most comfortable cells now at the bottom of the Atlantic Ocean. To divide the figures again, of the 159 Americans on board, 128 had perished and of the 129 children aboard the *Lusitania*, 94 perished; Included in that figure are 31 infants out of a total of 35 on board. Only four were saved.

An interesting footnote to Horgan's inquest is that it was originally scheduled for Monday, May 10th. When Vice Admiral Coke learned of it, he cabled Admiral Oliver in London and informed him. Oliver sent instructions that on no account was the hearing to proceed and above all, Captain Turner was not to testify under any circumstances.

Horgan must have somehow heard of this and he therefore brought it forward by two days. Upon closing the hearing, Horgan remarked that the Admiralty were "as belated on this occasion as they had been in protecting the *Lusitania*."

So ended the Kinsale inquiry. After a day of complete rest on Sunday, Will went straight to the Cunard superintendent at Queenstown, Captain Dodd, first thing Monday morning. He told Dodd that either more than one torpedo had hit the ship or that more likely, the one torpedo that he'd seen from the bridge had caused part of the cargo to explode. He also complained bitterly that the escort he'd been told to expect was not there to meet him. Will then made arrangements to leave Ireland and return to his home, a house called "NewHolme", in Ormskirk Road, Aintree, Liverpool.

The Perjurers...

Monday, May 10th, 1915. Admiralty House, Whitehall, London.

After truly Herculean efforts over the weekend, Admiral Oliver and Captain Richard Webb had finally managed to complete the official Admiralty version of the sinking of the *Lusitania*. Ultimately, Fisher had left it all to them. Churchill was due back from France that day and the Admiralty's case had now been fully prepared for his return and for the subsequent Board of Trade inquiry which was to be held in four weeks time. Presiding over the inquiry would be Lord Mersey.

Given that they both had the full facts of the disaster, Oliver and Webb resorted to a hatchet job, when they concocted, as opposed to constructed, the Admiralty's case. The first casualty was the truth; the second casualty was to have been Will Turner.

Oliver's problem was twofold. Firstly, the *Lusitania* had been successfully attacked by a German submarine, which the Admiralty KNEW to be operating in that area, after all measures to protect the ship had been withdrawn. Secondly, the *Lusitania* had gone down in a mere 18 minutes with terrible loss of life due to the explosive nature of the cargo which the Admiralty's Trade Division had loaded aboard her. If either or both of those facts were to become public knowledge, the buck would stop at the Admiralty. All sorts of awkward questions would be asked and heads would undoubtedly roll from the highest positions. The higher they fell from, the harder they would land. So, a scapegoat was needed urgently and who better than the *Lusitania's* Captain?

Oliver quite rightly reasoned that any inquiry would want to know the content and nature of any wireless instructions sent to the ship that day and what messages, if any, had been received from the ship. He now had all of those in his possession. He knew that up till she had received Vice Admiral Coke's instructions to divert into Queenstown, the *Lusitania* had been 25 miles from the South Coast of

Ireland. Oliver therefore removed all trace of Coke's signal from the final list of signals he prepared. Let Captain Turner explain why he'd suddenly decided to come close to the land.

Meanwhile, Captain Webb was busy tailoring the advices and instructions which Captain Turner may or may not have had.

Webb knew the instructions that Turner had been sent by wireless. Those that were on Oliver's list he could not alter as such. But he could alter the context in which they might be understood. For example; *"PASS HARBOURS AT FULL SPEED."* Now there was no longer a "divert" instruction, *Lusitania* could be said to have been passing Queenstown. If the fact that *Lusitania's* maximum speed had been reduced due to one boiler room being shut down was then omitted, how would it look for Turner, testifying that his ship was making only 18 knots, when she'd taken the Blue Riband at 24 knots in a blaze of publicity?

Then there was a part of the same signal that said *"STEER MID CHANNEL COURSE."* That piece actually referred to specific channels such as St George's Channel, North Channel or the English Channel. It did not refer to the Atlantic Ocean off the Old Head of Kinsale, which patently is not, and never has been, a Channel. But if one could simply call the distance between any two pieces of land "a channel," or even effectively rename the waters off southern Ireland "The Irish Channel", or "The Irish Sea", or even "The Celtic Sea"; then at 15 miles off Kinsale, *Lusitania* was not anywhere near the supposed "mid channel point." Webb then decided to say that *Lusitania* was only eight miles offshore and he also decided to say that eight miles offshore was her "usual trade route," which meant that Turner could now be said to have disregarded two further instructions, *"AVOID HEADLANDS"* and the advice to keep off the usual peacetime routes. It will be remembered that *Lusitania's* usual trade route was three miles offshore, but who was counting? Certainly not Webb.

Webb then discovered that an Admiralty advice dated April 16th, 1915, clearly recommended the Naval measure of Zig-Zagging to avoid a submarine attack. Further investigation revealed to Webb that although this advice was drafted on April 16th, it was not circulated to the various shipping companies till May 2nd at the earliest. Turner could not possibly have seen it as the *Lusitania* had only left New York the day before. However, Webb decided to include it in his report and emphasised the April 16th date to such a degree that anyone reading his report would assume that Turner had it in his possession for at least two weeks before his ship was sunk.

Webb had one last point to make in order to seal Captain Turner's fate. He had now conclusively "proved" that Captain Turner had PURPOSEFULLY IGNORED just about all his "instructions." He now had to say WHY Captain Turner had acted in this way. To that end, Webb neatly implied that Captain Turner was in the pay of the Germans. This inference was backed up by a report from Sir Cecil Spring-Rice, British Ambassador in Washington, on the subject of possible German infiltration of Cunard's New York offices. Sir Cecil's information came from Sir Courtenay Bennett and actually referred to the possibility of sabotage attempts by German or pro-German dockworkers in the port of New York. However, Webb simply left that bit out. Webb finished by suggesting that Turner probably thought he would have sufficient time to beach the *Lusitania* before she actually sank and therefore he may have thought that no lives would have been lost as a result of his "treachery."

Having concocted his case, Webb signed it and passed it on to Oliver, who added his list of carefully selected signals, initialled it and passed the whole lot to Fisher.

By the time Fisher had read it he was livid. At the end of the report he wrote "Fully Concur! As the Cunard Company would not have employed an incompetent man, the certainty is absolute that Captain Turner is not a fool but a Knave!" He expressed in the margins his profound hope that Captain Turner would be arrested immediately after the inquiry, whatever its outcome. Fisher then passed it on to Churchill to read.

Churchill didn't get around to reading it until late on Friday, May 14th, by which time the political climate was changing somewhat,

The Perjurers

due to a sensational report in *The Times* of the chronic shell shortage on the Western Front which, (indirectly), Churchill had a hand in. The correspondent who penned the article was in France the previous weekend with Churchill. It was part of Churchill's plan to extricate himself from the Admiralty. The aim was to topple Lord Kitchener, then temporarily step into his place. Churchill was also actively intriguing to remove the Foreign Secretary, Sir Edward Grey, from office and to supplant his own good friend, A. J. Balfour, in Grey's place. The report in *The Times* however, merely served to increase the considerable pressure already on Asquith's uneasy tenure at No. Ten. So in fact, Churchill had ultimately shot himself in the foot. The war council meeting that Friday morning had been a strained affair. Fisher was still harbouring a good deal of resentment with Churchill's name on it and the pair were at odds again over the Dardanelles.

It was against this background that Churchill read Webb's report. Either he realised the fact that his plan to topple Kitchener had backfired and was now threatening his own position, or possibly he just accepted Fisher's view to try to placate the Old Admiral. Having read it, Churchill made his own notes, adding; "Fully concur... I consider the Admiralty case against Captain Turner should be pressed before Lord Mersey by a skillful counsel, and that Captain Webb should attend as a witness, if not employed as assessor: We shall pursue the Captain without check."

Having been read by everybody, the file was returned to Captain Webb, who in turn forwarded it to Lord Mersey with a note pinned to it, which stated that the Board of the Admiralty considered it to be politically expedient that Captain Turner should be most publicly blamed for the disaster.

At home in Liverpool, Will Turner was still suffering from shock after the sinking. He didn't say much about it to Mabel and she knew him well enough not to ask. He'd tell her in his own good time, if he wanted to. Right now, he was best left alone. He was also mourning the death of his good friend Archie Bryce who, like most of the staff of the engineers department, was still at his post in the *Lusitania's* engine room.

When news of the disaster had first reached Will's mother, Charlotte, by way of a family friend, she said that she was "deeply distressed at the loss of so much life and of so fine a ship." Of her son she said, "Will most surely would come through. I know he will do his duty to the end, but I also know that he will never drown." Will had proved her correct by going to see her as soon as he'd arrived back in Liverpool.

A Damned Dirty Business...

Before Lord Mersey's inquiry was convened, Will Turner had to attend an interview with the Board of Trade's solicitors. Also present at the interview was a representative of the Admiralty. The details of Captain Webb's report were set out for him and he was told that at no time had he been ordered to divert into Queenstown. The Admiralty list of signals drawn up by Admiral Oliver was shown to him and he could see for himself that Coke's signal, the one sent to him in naval code, wasn't there. As all his papers, including the *Lusitania's* log and her signals register, had all gone down with the ship, there was nothing in Will's possession with which to counter Webb's allegations. The chart he'd saved, on it's own, would not be sufficient and he could hardly stand up in court and accuse such an august institution as the British Admiralty of lying without having overwhelming evidence to support him.

Now Will should have known exactly where he stood. They were going to blame him for the loss of his ship, the ship they had failed to protect, but he seems to have been unable to grasp this situation fully, as was evidenced by his manner at the inquiry.

The Cunard Company and Captain Turner were represented at the inquiry by Mr. Butler Aspinall, K. C. Whom had been selected by Cunard's lawyers Messrs. Hill. Dickinson and Co. He was to be assisted by two other barristers; a Mr. C. Lang K. C. and Mr A. H. Maxwell.

The barristers for the Board of Trade were; the Solicitor-General of England, Sir Frederick Smith; the Attorney-General, Sir Edward Carson with Mr. P. Branson and Mr. I. Dunlop to assist them. The solicitor to the Board of Trade was Sir Ellis Cunliffe.

On the bench, presiding, was H. M. Receiver of Wrecks, Lord Mersey, assisted by four naval assessors, two from the Royal Navy and two from the Merchant Navy.

One of the Royal Navy assessors needs to singled out at this juncture. He was Admiral Sir Frederick Inglefield, lately in overall command of the Auxiliary Coast Patrol, that force recently charged with the duty of protecting one RMS. *Lusitania.* Inglefield also deserves mention on another point. He was in sole possession of the master set of case documents prepared by the Admiralty. Sir Frederick Smith had the only other copy. We must mention this now because it was to have a direct bearing on the outcome of the inquiry.

The inquiry was convened at Central Hall, Westminster on June 15th, 1915. There were a total of seven hearings, only four of which were public, two were held "in camera", that it to say closed; and one was held unannounced at the Westminster Palace hotel.

We do not propose to cover the inquiry comprehensively as it was rather a drawn out affair and has, in any case, been amply covered in other books. What the readers of this book need to be reminded of is that Captain Webb had already asked Lord Mersey to blame Captain Turner for the disaster and also that one of his assessors, Admiral Sir Frederick Inglefield, had already been briefed, and instructed to find Captain Turner guilty of gross negligence if not treasonable behaviour.

Unknown of course to Lord Mersey was the fact that ALL the evidence had been carefully sifted and any references to explosions taking place forward of No. 1 funnel had been removed. Any passengers who had made statements which put the impact of the torpedo forward of the bridge, were not called to testify at the inquiry. Crew depositions were treated similarly, and for the rest, the Admiralty simply fashioned the questions to suit their requirements.

If Will Turner thought that he might have had an ace up his sleeve in the shape of the Marconi operator who had received the twelve-word message from Vice Admiral Coke, he was to be bitterly disappointed. Mr. McCormick was also not called to testify. Mr Leith, the Marconi operator who was on duty at the time of the attack but OFF duty at 11:02 hours when Coke's message came in, was called instead as he could truthfully confirm receipt of the LATER Admiralty messages. Will Turner was on his own.

The first day's hearings may best be described as a scene setter. The design and construction of the *Lusitania* was covered and then the attack upon and subsequent sinking of the ship was described. Captain Turner was called and was asked a total of 160 questions, mostly of general nature, with regard to the level of his experience as a Captain, whether the *Lusitania* had been armed and what had taken place during the sinking. He did cause a stir in answer to one question though.

Mr Cotter, representing some of the crew of the *Lusitania*, asked "Was the crew of the *Lusitania* proficient in handling the boats, in your estimation?" To which Will replied; "No, they were not." Mr Cotter then asked if that meant that the crew were incompetent, to which Will replied that they merely required a good deal more practice at lowering boats.

Captain Turner giving evidence at one of the public sessions of Lord Mersey's Inquiry

Lord Mersey

After then being questioned by Mr. Clem Edwards who was representing the National Sailors and Fireman's Union, on the subject of lifeboats, Will was questioned by Butler Aspinall.

Aspinall questioned him on the precautions he had taken upon entering the danger zone and then returned to the crew's proficiency at boat handling. It must be remembered of course that Aspinall was also representing the Cunard line as well as Captain Turner. It will be seen from the following dialogue that Aspinall's technique was to put Will Turner into the position of merely confirming what Aspinall wanted him to say. Aspinall: "I want you to explain that a little. Is it your view that modern ships with their greasers and their stewards and their firemen, sometimes do not carry the old-fashioned sailor that you knew of in the days of your youth?" Turner: "That is right." Aspinall: "And you preferred the man of your youth?" Turner: " Yes, and I prefer him yet." Thus Aspinall had demonstrated to the court that there was no suggestion of the crew's incompetence in boat handling, merely inefficiency.

It was the hearings that were held "In camera" which dealt with the important issues such as the cargo, wireless instructions, anti submarine measures and Captain Turner's actions. It was to be in this arena that Captain Turner was to have been thrown to the lions. The source of our information at this point in the story has largely been drawn from Colin Simpson's book, "*Lusitania*". This is due to the fact that there has been no full publication of the "In Camera" transcripts. The only complete account of what took place during those hearings is contained in Lord Mersey's private papers and the only author who has had access to those papers is Colin Simpson, by special permission of Lord Mersey's family.

From the start of the "In camera" hearings, the Admiralty strove to prove that they had kept Captain Turner informed at all times as to enemy submarines, that they had given him definite instructions and that he had deliberately disobeyed them, thereby placing his ship in grave danger, with the tragic result which the court was now addressing.

113

For Will Turner, it was all a nightmare. Alfred Booth, Cunard's Chairman observed, "Poor Will appears thoroughly bemused by the whole affair. He consistently clings to Aspinall for support."

His state of mind can perhaps be judged by a letter he sent to his dear friend, Miss Brayton, on 10th June, which read:

Dear Miss Brayton.

Just a few lines to thank you for your very kind letter. I am thankful to say that I have not felt any bad effects from my terrible experiences, but I grieve for the poor innocent people that lost their lives and for those that are left to mourn their dear ones loss.

Please excuse me saying more because I hate to think or speak of it.

Trusting you and yours are well

With kind regards yours very sincerely

(signed)W. T. Turner.

Initially, Aspinall was having an exasperating time trying to get Will to give answers of more than one word. Will could not, it seems, understand fully what the Admiralty were doing to him or why they were doing it. He was constantly confused about the evidence and gave his answers reluctantly. This of course only served to further the nature of the Admiralty's case against him. For example, when pressed on the question of the April 16th memo about zig-zagging, he reluctantly admitted that he must have seen it, although Aspinall later managed to drag it out of him after the memo had been read out in court for a second time:. "Now that it has been read to me again, it seems a different language." Of course it was! He was thinking of the February 10th advice note to steer a serpentine course if a submarine was sighted, which of course he had seen. But it was a useful round to his opponents initially.

The Admiralty had persuaded the court that although he'd been instructed to avoid headlands, he had deliberately come close inshore; he had disobeyed the instruction to pass harbours at full speed

114

and had in fact, by his own admission, reduced speed. He was not zig-zagging but steering a straight, undeviating course; nor was his ship in "mid-channel." As far as the Admiralty had ascertained "the vessel appears to have been on her usual trade route" and the only instruction the master appeared to have obeyed was to aim to make his port at dawn".

Lord Mersey had the list of signals, which he had been told was complete. No other signals had been sent. Though "of a general and negative nature," the court was further persuaded that they constituted specific warnings.

The only defence so far offered for his "incredible" actions was that he wanted to fix his position before entering St. George's Channel. Not very credible to the court, given the "wealth" of information and specific instructions said to have been in his possession. When pressed to reveal the nature of his Admiralty instructions, Turner could only respectfully refer the inquiry to the Admiralty, as he was not of course allowed to divulge any operational orders. The court was left to rely almost solely on Captain Webb's memorandum. It was not looking good for Will Turner.

Yet it was the court's reliance on Webb's dirty work which ultimately saved Will Turner.

Butler Aspinall concluded his case for Captain Turner's defence to the best of his abilities. He knew he was having to make the best of a bad job. He emphasised all the precautions that Will had taken before the *Lusitania* entered the danger zone. He admitted that the ship was not zig-zagging but did manage to convince Lord Mersey that Will had acted throughout with the safety of his passengers uppermost in his mind and that Will's policy had been one of passenger safety first, Admiralty advices second. As a finale, Aspinall read out a long list of the names of all the ships that had suffered the same fate as the *Lusitania*, in the same waters, within the six weeks previous to the *Lusitania's* sinking.

Next it was the turn of Sir Frederick Smith to sum up his case for the Admiralty and the Board of Trade. He concentrated on the signals which had been sent to the *Lusitania* and it was at this point that the Admiralty's case was scuppered.

Smith, during the course of his monologue, referred to a message which apparently told Captain Turner to avoid a particular area by keeping well off the land. Lord Mersey interjected because he could not find this message. Mersey asked Smith if he was reading from the Admiralty memorandum headed "*Lusitania.*" Smith confirmed that he was. Lord Mersey then called Smith to the bench and asked him to point it out on the copy Mersey had in front of him. Smith could not, for the simple reason that the message was not present on Mersey's copy.

Mersey then asked Aspinall to approach the bench and bring his copy with him. It was not on Aspinall's copy either. Aspinall thought it must be new evidence of which he and apparently Mersey, were unaware for some reason. Smith assured them that it was not new as he had been working from it throughout the proceedings.

Lord Mersey then leaned across and took Admiral Inglefield's file from him. Contained in Inglefield's file was the sending log of the Naval Wireless Station at Valentia. There on the log was Vice Admiral Coke's 12 - word signal to the *Lusitania*, in Naval code, timed at 11:02 hours on Friday, May 7th, 1915.

Mersey reacted instantly. Summoning the Crown Solicitor-General, Sir Ellis Cunliffe to the bench, Mersey coldly demanded an immediate explanation. Sir Ellis couldn't offer him a satisfactory reply. He asked Sir Ellis which was the correct file. Sir Ellis told him that Inglefield's was the master file so therefore the correct one.

If Mersey was angry at the discovery, Sir Frederick Smith was doubly so. "I do not want it," he said, referring to Inglefield's file. "I think it would be very unfair of me when this has not been put to the Master and has not been produced in evidence." He was now specifically referring to the 11:02 hours message in Naval Code sent to Captain Turner. Smith now realised he'd been conducting his 'Prosecution' on a basis of falsified evidence. He would proceed no further.

Lord Mersey was not slow to realise that the Admiralty had made a determined attempt to mislead his inquiry. Going back over the questions submitted by the Board of Trade, Mersey now realised that they had been specifically tailored for the given purpose of making Captain Turner appear negligent. This was especially so in the case of the question which asked whether or not any instructions had been sent to the Master of the *Lusitania* and whether those instructions had been carried out. The logical progression of the question is "what was the nature of those instructions?" But that question was of course, left out.

Mersey was now quietly seething. After a further discussion with the Counsels he decided to end the inquiry by simply adjourning it. He then asked the four assessors to give him their written opinions in separate sealed envelopes, as to Captain Turner's guilt. Only Admiral Sir Frederick Inglefield returned a verdict of guilty, the other three decided that Captain Turner was not to blame.

Inglefield, not happy that the scapegoat had escaped, complained about this 'Whitewashing' of Captain Turner to the secretary to the Admiralty. But there had been changes at the Admiralty during the course of the inquiry.

On May 15th, First Sea Lord Jacky Fisher had formally resigned. Fearing he would be made jointly to blame for the disaster which the Dardanelles campaign was fast becoming, he made a strategic withdrawal to Scotland. The shell shortage had turned into a government crisis and the only way out for Asquith and Co was a coalition. The Conservative Party's price for such was that First Lord of the Admiralty Winston Churchill, be sent into the political wasteland.

Churchill wasn't "sent to Coventry;" that at least was on the map. Churchill was sent to guard the Duchy of Lanchester, which wasn't on any map.

With a new Board of the Admiralty headed ironically by A. J. Balfour, Inglefield's complaint fell on deaf ears. The Admiralty had not only changed its body, it had changed its mind.

On July 17th, 1915 the court was assembled to hear the final verdict. The court found that "torpedoes fired by a submarine of German nationality" had caused the sinking of the *Lusitania*. The court opined that "this act was done not merely with the intention of sinking the ship, but also with the intention of destroying the lives of the people on board."

In the annex to his report, Lord Mersey stated that whilst Captain Turner may have disregarded some of the Admiralty's advices, he had most definitely followed his Admiralty instructions. The advices, said Lord Mersey, were "not intended to deprive him of the right to exercise his skilled judgement........." Lord Mersey went on to say that "he exercised his judgement for the best. It was the judgement of a skilled and experienced man, and although others may have acted differently............ He ought not, in my opinion, to be blamed."

Outside in the street, Alfred Booth and Captain Will Turner shook hands for the benefit of the press photographers who were present. The court had publicly exonerated Cunard and Captain Turner.

As Will and Mabel headed for Euston station to catch the train home for Liverpool, Will must have breathed a sigh of relief that it was all over. Perhaps now that he had been formally and publicly cleared of blame, the backhanded remarks from some members of the public would cease. He hadn't told Mabel about the white feather somebody had handed to him on his way into one of the earlier public hearings.

Given what Lord Mersey had discovered for himself during the course of his inquiry, it is hardly surprising that he should end this exhaustive hearing by merely concurring with the Kinsale coroner's verdict. Though he would not give the Admiralty their scapegoat, he did have to blame the Germans for this dastardly act.

So, the "beastly Hun" was found guilty and justice, at least to some, appeared to have been done. But it was a fundamentally unsound justice, as Lord Mersey knew only too well.

Two days after reaching his verdict, Lord Mersey waived his

fee for the case and formally resigned from his position as HM Receiver of Wrecks, stating that he no longer wished to serve. His last words on the subject were; "The *Lusitania* case was a damned, dirty business." But he did have one small consolation. However much they tried, now or in the future, the Admiralty would never be able to completely cover their tracks. Lord Mersey, in his wisdom, had confiscated the entire contents of Inglefield's master file.

With the inquiry over, things were left to settle down at Cunard. Ten days after the *Lusitania* had been sunk, Captain Dow had returned from his somewhat providential rest. He no doubt was counting his blessings, but at the same time, his heart went out to Will. "Fairweather Dow " had now taken command of the *Aquitania*. Dazzle painted, she was now serving as a troopship to the Dardanalles. *Mauretania* was being used for the same purpose.

Troopships and a New Years' Honour...

Alfred Booth had continued to be a friend to Will, retaining him as a standby or relief Captain. After the ordeals of the sinking and the inquiry, Booth thought it best to let Will have a quiet life for a while. It had all been particularly traumatic for Will and the discovery of Archie Bryce's body, washed ashore at the end of June, had not made things any easier. However, Will soon tired of the quiet life and yearned to go back to sea.

On October 25th, 1915, he was given command of the 8,845-ton freighter, *Ultonia*. The *Ultonia* was normally employed running from Hungary to New York via Gibraltar. However, she had been requisitioned for government service and Will was to take her to Quebec, there to embark Canadian troops. The troops were destined for France and once disembarked, Will brought the *Ultonia* back to England.

His next voyage was back to Quebec, which was as uneventful as the last voyage. As Will had some time on his hands, he decided to take the train down to New York.

Upon arrival in New York, he went to visit Mercedes and then a friend of his, a physician by the name of Edwin Sternberger, who later recalled that Will looked somewhat thinner, greyer in the hair and also that his eyes had lost some of their sparkle since the *Lusitania's* loss.

Ultonia's schedule was not a tight one and Will agreed to meet a reporter from the *New York Times* at Dr. Sternberger's house, for the purpose of an interview. Dressed in his uniform, he was photographed and they sat down to commence the interview.

He went to great pains to clear the names of those who had lost their lives and paid tribute to the crew, especially to those who had lost their lives whilst trying to save others. He particularly mentioned Staff

Captain Anderson in this respect. He flatly refused to divulge the nature of his Admiralty instructions and maintained that "the submarines would have got her as they planned," no matter what course of action he'd taken. The rest of the interview bore a close resemblance to the Admiralty's version of events. This is hardly surprising as they constantly drummed it into him both before and during the inquiry. Will always publicly maintained that there were two submarines waiting for the *Lusitania*; One off Fastnet and one off Conningbeg. Referral back to the signals he'd received prior to the attack will explain his belief in this, even though we now know that only *U-20* was in the area. Having obtained their story, the newspapermen left.

The following Saturday, a table had been reserved for Captain Turner and his guest, Dr. Sternberger, at Luchow's on East 14th Street. It was almost like old times. August Luchow welcomed them as they arrived and personally showed them to their table. Luchow expressed his regret at the loss of the *Lusitania*, but hoped that "Herr Kapitan" would not hold it against him just because he happened to be German. Will had always enjoyed the atmosphere at Luchow's but this time it seemed different. It was because there was no *Lusitania* at the Cunard pier at the other end of the street.

The next morning, he took the train back to his ship and set sail for France to disembark the troops he was carrying. He never set foot in New York again.

On December 13th, 1916 whilst offloading, the *Ultonia* grounded in St. Nazaire roads. She was successfully refloated with assistance and without damage. On Christmas Eve, Will took her out to Canada again and upon his return was once more without a ship as *Ultonia* was released from government service

It was in fact another nine months before Will got a ship again. This time it was the 7,907-ton, *Ausonia*. He commanded her for three round voyages to Canada and then on December 27th, 1916 a curious twist of fate saw him rushed to the Mediterranean under strangely similar circumstances to those which put him in command of the *Lusitania* for her fateful voyage.

He took command of another of his old ships the 14,067-ton *Ivernia* again. A former Mediterranean service passenger liner, she had been converted in September of 1914 to an armed troopship. Her current Captain was Arthur Rostron, a friend of Will's and famous, it will be recalled, for rescuing the survivors of the *Titanic* disaster.

It is often said that Rostron had fallen ill and that Turner took over as a result. This is only partly true. Rostron was not ill, but in fact on an Admiralty anti submarine course. He was to spend a short time in a British submarine so as to get the feel of how a U-boat operated. They would approach a merchant ship whilst submerged and Rostron would be able to study the ship's behaviour through the submarine's periscope. The idea was to make merchant Captains aware of what potentially easy targets their ships presented to U-boat Commanders. The idea of course was secret, so he "went sick" in order to attend the course. And most prophetic it would turn out to be.

Will took *Ivernia* out of Salonika on New Year's Day, 1917 with 2,800 troops on board destined for the port of Alexandria. Mindful of his previous experience, the *Ivernia* was steering an irregular zig-zag course. All appeared to be going well when later that same day, 58 miles off Cape Matapan, Kapitan-Leutnant Steinbauer commanding the German Submarine *UB-47* managed to put a torpedo into the *Ivernia*. Fortunately, the *Ivernia* did not sink quite as rapidly as the *Lusitania* had done, though 87 troops and 36 members of *Ivernia*'s crew died. Will Turner was washed off the bridge as the ship sank. He clung to a chair with a sense of Deja vu until he was rescued. The *Ivernia* was Will Turner's last command.

October of 1917 saw the spectre of the *Lusitania* rise again. Will was summoned by American Judge Julius B. Mayer, as a principal witness in the United States own *Lusitania* inquiry. Again it was Butler Aspinall who represented him, but this time it was a little different. The "hearing" was simply a question and answer session, which was held in London. A Mr. Scanlan represented the Americans and once again the nature of the Admiralty instructions was the main subject of the questions. Once again Will referred them to the Admiralty,

122

refusing to be drawn. The matter was dropped. For the rest of the evidence, the transcripts of the PUBLIC hearings of the Mersey inquiry were used. Not surprisingly, Judge Mayer came to the same verdict as that of Lord Mersey. But then, America had now entered the war on the allied side.

In the New Years Honours List for 1918, the entry in the London Gazette reads; "Captain W. T. Turner. - was the commander of the *Lusitania* when that vessel was torpedoed, and he afterwards went to sea again in charge of a ship on Government service, which also was torpedoed by a German Submarine. He again took service in another ship, of which he is still acting as Master."

Alfred Booth, now Sir Alfred Booth, had recommended Will for the rank of Officer of the Most Excellent Order of the British Empire, an honour newly created by King George VI, in recognition of his subjects war services of a non combatant nature. The position of Officer in this order of knighthood is the fourth of the five ranks within the order. The first two ranks are positions of knighthood, then come the ranks of Commander, Officer and finally, Member. There is also a lower class for those who are ineligible for the other classes. Those recipients would receive the Empire Medal.

Honouring Will Turner at Alfred Booth's behest was also possibly 'one in the eye' for the Admiralty, after their thoroughly discreditable attempts to blame Will for the loss of the *Lusitania*. The announcement of Will's OBE was also posted in Lloyds List of January 11th, 1918. Will accepted the honour as a measure of Alfred Booth's personal faith and friendship.

The final shot of the First World War was fired shortly before 11 am on November 11th, 1918. It was now "All quiet on the Western Front," and indeed on every other front. During the conflict, more than ten million lives had been lost and Cunard had lost 22 of their ships

Retirement…

In October of 1919, Will retired from Cunard after a total of 34 years service under the Cunard flag. He told Mabel that the only thing he wanted now was a quiet life. To that end Will and Mabel moved house.

They bought a large detached house in Westella Road, Yelverton, Devon, which they again called "NewHolme" and where Will took up beekeeping. Close to Dartmoor, this was very much Mabel's country. But even here, folk soon learned who was living in their midst. They also discovered that the Captain wasn't one to make social calls either. They would have to go to him. It was not long till the inevitable journalists started calling either. Not much chance of the quiet life after all.

On March 30th, 1920, Will's mother Charlotte died at the grand old age of 90. She was laid to rest at Rake Lane cemetery and it was shortly after this that Will decided to move back to Liverpool. He felt much happier on his own ground.

They house they moved into was No. 50, De Villiers Avenue, Great Crosby. A spacious three bedroom, semi detached house in a quiet suburb of Liverpool. Will had a flagpole erected in the garden and on special days such as St. George's day or the King's birthday, he flew the Union Jack from it. He was like a favourite uncle to most of the local children. They would come into the garden and play with Will's dog and his cat, whilst Will played his fiddle and taught them the sea shanties he'd learned as a deck hand in sailing ships.

In 1921, Winston Churchill's book THE WORLD CRISIS was published. Despite being originally four volumes in length, it sold well and was given much credence at first issue. The section relating to the sinking of the *Lusitania* can be best described as a slightly more silver-tongued retelling of Captain Webb's version of events. It was the publication of this book which brought journalists to Will Turner's door again.

In the late 1920's, Will went to Australia for 18 months to try to find his two sons, Norman and Percy, whom he had not seen since the Mersey inquiry. His estranged wife had emigrated to Australia and his sons had gone with her. His search however, was unsuccessful. It was at this time that Will was first diagnosed has having cancer of the intestines. Possibly it was this knowledge which drove him to seek his sons, 12,500 miles away.

In 1930, Will Turner was admitted to hospital for an operation to remove some of the cancerous growth from his stomach. It was evidently decided that the cancer was incurable, as he had no further surgery.

In the summer of 1932, a more welcome visitor came to see Will Turner. Knocking at the door of 50, De Villiers Avenue, he introduced himself to Mabel as Albert Bestic, a former officer of the Captain's. Mabel asked him to wait, as the Captain was not in the best of health. Upon returning to Bestic in the hallway she informed him that the Captain had said that he had never heard of him.

Bestic was just about to leave when he remembered something. Turning to Mabel on the doorstep he said, "Just a minute, would you tell him my name is really Bisset?" Mabel duly did as she was asked and returned a few moments later looking a little embarrassed. "What did he say?" asked Bestic. Mabel replied, "He said, why the hell didn't he say so in the first place?!" Mabel let him into the lounge.

In his armchair sat an emaciated old man, a mere shadow of his former self. Nothing remotely like the brisk Commodore of the Cunard line that Bestic remembered. But when Will looked up at him, Bestic saw those eyes and fought back a strange compunction to snap to attention. "Is that you, Bisset?" The old man asked. "It is sir," replied Bestic. "Of course, I remember now. That woman must have got your name wrong. Well, what certificates have you got?" It sounded more like an order than a friendly question. "Square rig Master, sir," said Bestic. The old man grunted his approval. He'd been right about "Bisset".

50 De Villiers Avenue, Great Crosby, Merseyside

Will managed to light his pipe and as he sat back in his chair, he started to tell Bestic about his days in sail. The *Grasmere*, *White Star*, his first time round the Horn, the time he fell overboard from the *Thunderbolt* and his first command, the *Star of the East*.

Bestic listened intently to his former Captain. "Good days, Bisset, good days" said Will as he came to the end of his reminiscences. Bestic saw his opening and asked Will if he had ever thought that the *Lusitania* had been in real danger that morning before she was attacked. "Naturally, I was worried," Will told him, "but I thought we had an even chance of escaping. The Admiralty didn't seem to be over concerned about it at the time so I reasoned that they must think there wasn't much danger. Gave me a false confidence. I wasn't given a fair deal, Bisset. It was a good two years afterward that they started to issue specific instructions." Will paused as a somewhat bitter expression crossed his face. "They said later that I should have steered a mid-channel course. With my ship in the Atlantic!" Will snapped his fingers in contempt. "No Bisset, I wasn't given a fair deal at all!"

Bestic then proceeded to tell Will that there was a proposed salvage expedition to the *Lusitania*. Bestic was working for them but they were having trouble locating the wreck. The official Admiralty position was eight miles off the Old Head of Kinsale. Will smiled ruefully and from the bookcase next to him produced the chart he'd stuffed inside his tunic before the *Lusitania* sank. "Wouldn't believe all the Admiralty tell you, Bisset," he said as he gave him the chart. He asked Bestic to retrieve his sextant from his day cabin for him if it was possible.

At that point, Mabel entered the room with Will's medication. "It's time for your medicine Captain," she said. Will mumbled something about a "damned petticoat government." But he took the medicine anyway. "All right fore and aft," he said to Bestic, "but my longitudinal bulkhead's given way!" A referral to the design layout of the *Lusitania's,* watertight bulkheads that proved to be a fatal design flaw.

'Bisset'- Albert Bestic (pictured in later years)

Bestic took his leave of the Captain and went back to the salvage company with the chart. Later exploration revealed the wreck to be 11.2 miles off the Old Head and within two miles of the position marked on Will's chart, which only showed the ship's course up to the point she was struck. She had travelled a further two and a half miles before she finally sank.

128

The last voyage of Captain Turner...

On Friday June 23rd, 1933, Will Turner died peacefully in his bed at home in 50, De Villiers Avenue. His funeral was held at Rake Lane Cemetery in Wallasey, Wirral, the following Monday, at 11:00 hours. The Rev. A. P. Miller of St. Lukes, Crosby, officiated as Will's coffin, draped with a Union Jack, was carried by six Cunard Quartermasters in full uniform, up to the Turner family grave. Also present were several surviving crewmen of the *Lusitania* and various inmates of the Mariner's Home in Wallasey who had previously served with Will. Cunard was also largely represented.

So ended the life of a truly remarkable man; laid to rest with his parents and his sister, in a cemetery on the banks of the River Mersey from where it all began.

Rather ironically, one year after Will's death, Cunard and their great rival the White Star Line, were forced to merge at the behest of the British Government, to become the Cunard-White Star Line and another world war with Germany, who by that time had perfected the U-boat with devastating results, was only five years away.

The last Voyage of Captain Turner

EPILOGUE...

Writing the story of a man's life more than sixty-five years after his death is not an easy task. In the case of major celebrities it is not usually too much of a problem as their lives tend to be fairly well documented, but in the case of someone like Captain Will Turner, gaps are bound to appear. We have done our best to fill them in where they occur, without resorting to fiction or mere supposition. Where gaps still occur, they have been left. There is nothing contained in this book which has not been verified by sight of documentary evidence.

It would seem that dates are the most common mistake to be made. Even the date of his birth on the family gravestone at Rake Lane Cemetery is incorrect. It shows the year of his birth as 1857 when in fact he was born in 1856.

The Liverpool newspapers followed his later career avidly, yet you will find that there are several slightly different versions of the same events, be they the rescues he took part in, awards made to him or of course, the *Lusitania* disaster.

And speaking of the disaster, there are so many versions of that, true and false, that it can be hard to know which to believe. On that note, we consider the book *"Lusitania"* by Colin Simpson to be the one to read. Whilst Colin Simpson's book does seem to dwell rather too long on the supposed plot by Churchill to deliberately place the *Lusitania* in harm's way, a theory which really does not stand up to competent investigation, no account can be one hundred per cent accurate, but we would still venture to say that Simpson's work is to the *Lusitania*, what Walter Lord's "A Night To Remember," is to the *Titanic*. Also well worth a read is the relevant section of Commander Patrick Beesley's "Room 40. British Naval Intelligence." He concedes that the Admiralty lied but he also perpetuates one or two of their lies. However, his account does examine the precautions that the Admiralty

132

could, and indeed should, have taken to protect the *Lusitania* and that in itself is most enlightening.

We have refrained from going into great detail about the loss of the *Lusitania* simply because ours is not a "*Lusitania*" book. Ours is a book about the man who was her Captain. Yet there are certain aspects of the disaster that cannot be wholly separated from the story of Will Turner.

In our reconstruction of fateful Friday we have presented the situation and events to you as Will saw them. We have given you the same information he had at the same points in the story. Our aim was to put the reader in exactly the same situation Will Turner was in so that his decisions and subsequent actions would be familiar to you. Given the situation he faced in the waters off Southern Ireland that day, would you have acted differently if the burden of command had rested with you? Personally, we think not, but you must remember not to judge the situation with hindsight.

Many 'experts' over the years have offered their own theories as to the course of action Will Turner should have taken that day, but it must always be borne in mind that hindsight is perfect vision; it is always easy to be wise after the event.

The other point we'd like to make is that the information Will had was undoubtedly bad. *U-20*'s position as given to him by the Admiralty was 20 miles South of the Conningbeg Lightship, when in fact it was known at the Admiralty that *U-20* was no longer in that vicinity. The Submarine off Fastnet never existed and Will was also told to expect an armed escort, HMS *Juno*, which unknown to him had been withdrawn. It must also be recalled that the deployment AND NAVIGATION of the *Lusitania* was the responsibility of the Admiralty, under the terms of their 1914 requisitioning of the ship.

As to the reasons why such a well found ship should sink in a mere 18 minutes after only one, G-type torpedo struck her, we would refer you once again to Colin Simpson's excellent book and also Patrick Beesley's book, "Room 40. British Naval Intelligence 1914-1918". The only thing we'd like to mention on that score is that contrary to a more modern theory proffered by Dr. Robert Ballard that it was the coal dust which exploded and sank her, we do not believe this was the case.

For Dr. Ballard's theory to hold water he contends that Schwieger's torpedo struck *Lusitania's* in one of her coalbunkers, which he states were virtually empty of everything but a thick layer of inflammable dust. This was not so. *Lusitania* had been bunkered to capacity with a FULL supply of coal when she left New York. It will be remembered that coal was cheaper there and it will also be recalled that Booth had granted Will won the concession from Alfred Booth on the grounds that full bunkers would also solve the worst of *Lusitania's* ballasting problem. Another point worthy of mention is that with *Lusitania* having a FULL supply of coal but running with one boiler room shut down, there was no way her bunkers would have been anywhere near empty at the time she was attacked.

Schwieger's torpedo actually found its mark in the forward cargo hold. The site of impact can be fairly accurately placed by three pieces of evidence. Firstly, Schwieger's log. It will be remembered that in fact, he revised his initial observations. Having overestimated the speed of his target, he realised that his shot had struck the ship further forward of where he had first thought. Secondly, Able Seaman Thomas Quinn, one of the lookouts in the crow's nest at the time of the attack, stated in his mandatory deposition to the Board of Trade that the torpedo struck the ship on the "Starboard side, abaft the foremast." The word "abaft" is a nautical term, which means "immediately aft of". We know that Schwieger set the running depth of his torpedo at three metres, which is about ten feet. So the impact area was behind the foremast and ten feet below the waterline.

On the deck plans of the *Lusitania*, you would be looking therefore to place the impact somewhere between frames 251 and 256 and ten feet below the waterline. This area is the top of the forward hold (aft end, starboard side) and immediately below the baggage room. Which brings us to our third piece of evidence. There were no survivors at all from the baggage room working party and had he not stopped to change his uniform, then Bestic would have perished in there too.

Also of interest is the assertion that Captain Turner should have called out the off duty stokehold watch and lit up those boilers which were shut down, thereby raising steam for 25 knots. At that speed, no submarine could have caught the *Lusitania*.

Tempting theory that one, isn't it? It was put forward by the Admiralty of all people. It sounds such an easy and obvious thing to do, doesn't it? So why didn't they send Captain Turner a signal on Thursday, May 6th, ordering him to do exactly that? The danger by then was staring the Admiralty in the face. Although it would have taken fully 20 hours to light that section of boilers and to raise a full head of steam, (and it must be remembered that Archie Bryce was short of the 90 men required to man the closed boiler room) it may well have been possible to sustain 25 knots for the last leg of the journey. However, this would also have necessitated steering much further out into the Atlantic to avoid arriving at Liverpool too early to cross the bar. It would also have meant having to fix his position BEFORE commencing his high-speed run. But the real point that is overlooked in this theory is that the submerged U-boat travelling at nine knots wasn't the real enemy. The real enemy was the G-Type torpedo it fired, with it's 440lb warhead, streaking toward the target at some 38 knots.

By midnight on May 6th/7th the Admiralty knew of EVERY sinking and attack that *U-20* had made in the previous three days. They could also, had it been so desired, have sent any or all of the four modern, fast, 'L' Class destroyers out from Milford Haven to screen her and at *Lusitania's* maximum speed of 25 knots, those destroyers still had ten knots in hand. Instead, HMS *Lucifer*, *Linnet* and *Laverock* lay idle at their moorings while *Lusitania* went to the bottom. The point in all this is that the Admiralty were in a good position to take some very positive action. They chose instead to do only things of a "general and negative nature", if they did anything at all. The only truly viable alternative was to have diverted the *Lusitania* around the

135

Western Irish coast to approach Liverpool by way of the North Channel. But this judgement is of course made with the benefit of hindsight.

The *Lusitania* held a special place in Will Turner's heart. Together, the *Lusitania*, Will Turner and Archie Bryce the chief engineer, were a winning team. But that team was shattered forever by Kapitan-Leutnant Walther Schwieger's torpedo. It was as if half of Will's life had been shattered too.

As if the disaster itself were not enough of an ordeal to go through, Will then had to suffer the Admiralty's public attempts to blame him for the loss of his ship; the very ship they were supposed to have protected.

Captain Webb's thoroughly despicable concoction of lies, half truths and twisted facts has had a remarkable effect. Even today there are responsible journalists, article writers, makers of television programmes, authors and even historians, all of whom really should know better, who simply retrieve a copy of Captain Webb's infamous memorandum from the Admiralty files in the Public Records Office and treat it as gospel. After a quick check in Winston Churchill's THE WORLD CRISIS they put pen to paper and perpetuate the falsities. A stupendous example of this can be found in a book entitled "The *Lusitania* Disaster: An episode in modern warfare and diplomacy." This book wholeheartedly condemns Captain Turner's actions on Fateful Friday, especially in the matter of "avoiding headlands". In order to support their claims, the book's authors, Thomas Bailey and Captain Paul Ryan, USN. Retired, called upon the opinion of Captain John C. Jamison, then Commodore of the American Line at the time of the writing of their book. Captain Jamison stated; "Four point bearings off the Old Head of Kinsale are unnecessary, unless the ship were making for Queenstown." – Quite. Bailey and Ryan were of course maintaining the Admiralty lie that the *Lusitania* was passing Queenstown, not diverting into Queenstown. This despite Schwieger's statement in *U-20*'s log that "the ship turns to starboard then takes a course to Queenstown". In the light of what we know

136

today, Jamison's statement can now only serve to underline the correctness of Turner's actions at that time. The rest of the book's treatment of Will Turner simply reiterates and supports Captain Webb's allegations against him, so furthering Webb's original purposes. As character assassinations go, Captain Webb's handiwork has been a "duesy"; it is over 84 years old and is still going strong.

What is seemingly forgotten, or never realised, is that the Admiralty's case against Captain Turner was concocted with the sole aim of shifting the responsibility for the deaths of 1,201 men, women and children away from where it truly belongs; laid at the respective feet of the British and American governments of the day, as well as the Admiralty and Kapitan-Leutnant Walther Schwieger.

One of the many things we hope you have come to understand through reading this book is that Captain William Turner was at the pinnacle of a very distinguished career when the *Lusitania* was sunk; a career which was hallmarked throughout with his remarkable sagacity. One only has to glance at his record; sterling service, devotion to duty, selfless courage, precision shiphandling and above all, pride in his profession. Look at how his crews loved him, taking a hitherto unknown pride in their ship. Look at how passengers flocked to his ships, creating for him a personal following among the wealthy and influential travellers without his even trying to. Will Turner was always a rather difficult man to get to know, but underneath that cool, aloof exterior, was a surprising warmth that, once discovered, was forever enjoyed by those who could count themselves as being among his friends.

Tragedy indeed that such a remarkable man should end his days as a virtual recluse, unable to bear the public scorn for his Admiralty inferred criminality in the loss of his ship.

Quite why nobody has decided to tell Will Turner's story until now is probably due to the ship eclipsing the man. The same is true of E. J. Smith, Captain of the ill-fated *Titanic*. Since 1958 there has been a plethora of books about this ship, but it is only recently that a biography of *Titanic*'s Captain has appeared.

Material for this book was drawn from both sides of the Atlantic, particularly in relation to his niece, Mercedes Desmore. She went on to become an accomplished actress, most notably in the United States.

The city of New York has changed a good deal since the *Lusitania* left for the last time. Pier 54 still stands today, though in a state of dereliction. The large Cunard transit shed that stood atop the pier was demolished in 1990 after a survey revealed it was on the point of collapse. Pier 54 has been given a new deck and currently awaits its planned redevelopment as a museum to historic shipping, surrounded by a large park.

Luchow's Restaurant at 110, East 14th Street, no longer exists. Having survived prohibition and two World Wars, it could not survive the 1970s decline of Union Square. By the 1980s, the once famous building was boarded up and empty, as were most properties in that area. Efforts to have a preservation order placed upon the building were unsuccessful and it was finally pulled down in 1995, after a somewhat suspicious fire.

As for Will's two sons, Norman died of old age, but Percy's fate was, in an odd way, related to the *Lusitania*. Percy, it will be recalled, had joined the Merchant navy. During the Second World War, he was serving as an intelligence officer. He died when a German U-boat torpedoed the ship he was travelling on. The attack took place off the Old Head of Kinsale and his ship sank less than one mile from the wreck of the *Lusitania*.

The fate of the man who put the *Lusitania* on the bottom is also worth recording at this point. In July of 1917, Kapitan Leutnant Walther Schwieger was admitted to the German empire's elite order of Knights, the "Ordre Pour Le Merite", in recognition of his having sunk a total of 190,000 tons of allied shipping. Despite having a French name, this ancient Prussian order of knighthood, created by King Frederick I of Prussia in 1667, was among the most distinguished orders in the world. It was given a French title for two reasons; firstly because the order was structured along very similar lines to the world renowned French "Legion d' Honneur", due to King Frederick's love of all things French, and secondly to distinguish the order from all other German orders. Members of this noble order wore the Pour Le Merite medal, or "Blue Max" as it was more popularly known, which was Germany's highest award for gallantry in the face of an enemy. Schwieger's distinguished fellow members included future "Desert Fox" Erwin Rommel, air aces Manfred Von Richtofen, (the "Red Baron"), his younger brother Lothar, Max Immelmann, Oswald Boelcke and future Luftwaffe chiefs Ernst Udet and Hermann Goring.

The commendation for Schwieger's award made no mention at all of the sinking of his largest victim, the *Lusitania*. He was, by virtue of being a holder of this coveted award, officially a U-boat ace, ranking sixth in the league table of U-boat Commanders. He died with his entire crew, six weeks after receiving his medal, when in command of the U-88. Whilst being pursued by the Q-ship HMS *Stonecrop*, *U-88* struck a British laid mine off the island of Terschelling in the North Sea, on September 5th, 1917. He was 32 years of age when his worst nightmare came true.

After Will Turner died, Mabel Every sold 50, De Villiers Avenue and moved in with her brother nearby. Will's estate was valued at £4,427,0s 9d and in his last will and testament, he named his bank manager, George Ball of Martin's Bank Ltd, Birkenhead; as executor, leaving the sum of £20 to him for his services in connection therewith. He left a further £100 to Josephine Cathroll, the nurse who had also helped to care for him since his operation, and the rest of his estate was left solely to Mabel Every for her "unremitting care and attention." He also left all of his personal belongings to her. The will was drawn up by Mr. Sydney J. Hill, of Hill, Dickinson & Co. Cunard's lawyers.

Journalists still tried to extract a story from Mabel, but the only thing she would say to them was, "No use asking me. All I can tell you is that the Captain followed his orders." If Will Turner ever did tell her the exact nature of those orders, and it seems likely that he probably did; Mabel kept his confidences to herself. She died in 1978, a spinster in an old folks' home.

50, De Villiers Avenue, Great Crosby, still stands today and until quite recently, so did the flagpole. At the time of writing, the house is owned by a very gracious lady by the name of Mrs. Lambert, who was kind enough to allow us inside Captain Turner's former home, and to photograph it. However, Mrs. Lambert has absolutely no desire to open her house to the public.

The last resting place of the Turners is of course the family grave in Rake Lane cemetery, Wallasey, Wirral, Merseyside. It is an unpretentious grave with a standard headstone that bears a long inscription, the full text of which reads:

" IN LOVING MEMORY OF CHARLES TURNER
(MASTER MARINER)
BORN 28th DECEMBER 1826. DIED 5th OCTOBER 1900.
ALSO CHARLOTTE NEE JOHNSON,
HIS WIFE
BORN 9th JANUARY 1830. DIED 30th MARCH 1920.
ALSO ANNIE MARIA,
THEIR DAUGHTER
BORN 18th FEBRUARY 1854. DIED 13th NOVEMBER 1913. ALSO
CAPT. WILLIAM THOMAS TURNER
O.B.E. R.N.R.
THEIR SON,
COMMODORE OF THE CUNARD S.S. LINE,
WHO WAS IN COMMAND OF THE R.M.S. *LUSITANIA* WHEN SHE WAS
TORPEDOED 7th MAY 1915. BORN 23rd OCTOBER 1857. DIED 23rd
JUNE 1933.

"FAITHFUL UNTO DEATH."

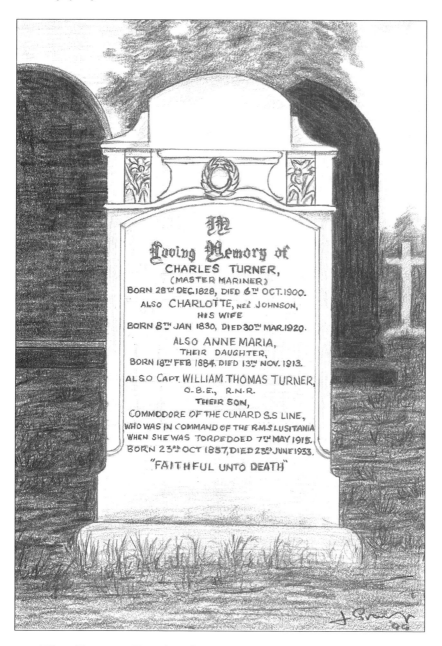

The Turner Family Grave, Wallasey, Merseyside

141

As previously mentioned, the year of Will's birth and that of his father's, is incorrect.

However, we think it fit to leave the last words about Will Turner to someone who actually knew the man. Whilst researching for this book, we came across a volume in the library of the National Maritime Museum at Greenwich, London, entitled "FAMOUS SHIPWRECKS".

The *Lusitania* is of course mentioned so we looked it up as the book was quite old. The book's author, Captain Frank H. Shaw, himself holder of an Extra Master's certificate, had this to say:

"As regard her Commander, Captain Turner, no praise can be too high for his qualities. I knew him personally; indeed, it was my fortune to sail shipmates with him in a more peaceful period; and I know that he was a very Bertrand du Guesclin of the Atlantic; a fearless knight, widely versed in the problems of the sea, and especially the treacherous Atlantic; and never one to lose his head in any emergency, however dire. The ill-fated Cunarder could not have been commanded by a better man........ To sum up the quality of her commander, it can be said that he was worthy of his beautiful ship."

Captain William Thomas Turner was as fine a Captain as ever paced a bridge; a gallant and extraordinary seaman who for more than 80 years has been the victim of a gross injustice. May he now forever rest in peace; with his name eternally cleared.

[PROBATE]

BE IT KNOWN that   WILLIAM THOMAS TURNER

of 50 De Villiers Avenue, Crosby near Liverpool in the

County of Lancaster,

died   there   on the   23rd   day of   June   19 33

AND BE IT FURTHER KNOWN that at the date hereunder written
the last will and Testament

of the said deceased was proved and registered in the District Probate Registry
of His Majesty's High Court of Justice at   LIVERPOOL
and that administration of all the estate which by law devolves to and vests
in the personal representative of the said deceased was granted by the
aforesaid Court to
          GEORGE BALLof 7 Palm Grove, Birkenhead

in the County of Chester, Bank Manager, the sole Executor

named in the said Will

Dated the   31ˢᵗ   day of   July   1933

Gross value of Estate   ... £ 4427. 0. 9.
Net value of Personal Estate £ 3499. 18.0.

205a.   Extracted by   Sydney J Hill, Solicitor Liverpool.

Above and overleaf:
The Last Will and Testament of Captain William
Thomas Turner.

MY WILL

THIS IS THE LAST WILL of me WILLIAM THOMAS TURNER of

50 De Villiers Avenue, Crosby, Liverpool 23. I appoint

Mr George Ball, Manager of Martins Bank Ltd Birkenhead

Branch, sole Executor of this my Will and I bequeath

to him the sum of (£20) twenty pounds To my maid I

bequeath (£100) One hundred pounds for her great help

in nursing me during my illness Her name is Josephine

Cathroll. To my housekeeper Mabel Every for her

unremitting care of me and attention of me, particularly

during my illness for the last three years after my

operation, and during the last 24 years I give and

bequeath all real and personal property I may die

possessed of absolutely and I revoke all former Wills or

Codicils.

Dated this 18th day of March1933.

Signed by the Testator, in the presence of us, both

present at the same time, and in the presence of each

other, have hereunto set our names as witnesses.

W.T. TURNER

Witness L.I. TAYLOR spinster

18 College Rd., Gt Crosby

15.4.33

"   D.E.M. TAYLOR spinster 18 College Road Gt Crosby

3 folios.

Affidavit filed that Will was duly

executed on the15th day of April 1933

J.C. Bromfield

District Registrar.

On the 31st day of July 1933

Probate of this Will was granted at

Liverpool

Certified to be a correct copy

Bibliography...

A NIGHT TO REMEMBER by Walter Lord.

ARMED MERCHANT CRUISERS by Kenneth Poolman.

THE BLUE RIBAND OF THE ATLANTIC by Tom Hughes.

LUSITANIA by Colin Simpson.

ROOM 40. BRITISH NAVAL INTELLIGENCE 1914-1918 by Patrick Beesley.

THE WORLD CRISIS by Winston Churchill.

EXPLORING THE LUSITANIA by Dr. Robert Ballard.

THE GREAT NAVAL RACE by Peter Padfield.

FAMOUS SHIPWRECKS by Captain Frank H. Shaw.

HOME FROM THE SEA by Sir Arthur Rostron.

ROUND THE HORN BEFORE THE MAST by Basil Lubbock.

THE CUNARD STORY by Howard Johnson.

MERCHANT FLEETS IN PROFILE by Duncan Haws.

SEVEN DAYS TO DISASTER by Des Hickey and Gus Smith.

LLOYDS REGISTER OF SHIPPING by Lloyds of London.

LLOYDS REGISTER OF SHIPS CAPTAINS by Lloyds of London.

BRITISH VESSELS LOST AT SEA by HMSO.

THE DEVIL'S DEVICE by Edwyn Gray.

JANE'S FIGHTING SHIPS 1914 by Jane's.

BOARD OF TRADE REPORT INTO THE LOSS OF THE S.S. LUSITANIA by HMSO.

THE FIRST WORLD WAR by Martin Gilbert.

BRITISH MERCHANT SHIPS SUNK BY U-BOATS IN THE 1914-1918 WAR by A J. Tennent.

THE MOST FORMIDABLE THING by Admiral William Jameson.

ASQUITH by Roy Jenkins.

TITANIC VOYAGER By Patrick Stenson.

THE LUSITANIA DISASTER: An episode in modern warfare and diplomacy by Thomas Bailey and Captain Paul Ryan USN. Retired.

MEDALS AND RIBBONS by H. Taprell Dorling.

THE BRITISH HONOURS SYSTEM by Lt. Cdr. J.H.B. Bedells. JP Hon. FHS. RN.

THE QUEEN'S ORDERS OF CHIVALRY by Brigadier Sir Ivan De la Bere.

Periodicals and Newspapers

DAILY MAIL

THE SHIPPING WORLD AND HERALD OF COMMERCE

LIVERPOOL COURIER

THE SHIPPING GAZETTE

THE JOURNAL OF COMMERCE, LIVERPOOL AND LONDON

LIVERPOOL POST AND MERCURY

NEW YORK TRIBUNE

NATIONAL GEOGRAPHIC

THE LONDON GAZETTE

CLEVELAND LEADER

LIVERPOOL WEEKLY STAR

NEW YORK TIMES

LLOYDS LIST

Appendix...

All the places where Captain Turner is known to have lived.

From 1856 to 1869 - Clarence St. Everton, Liverpool.
From 1869 to circa 1895 - Mostly away at sea, but still based at above address.
Circa 1896 to 1906 - 31, Springfield Rd. Sale, Manchester.
From 1906 to 1919 - "NewHolme", Ormskirk Rd. Aintree, Liverpool.
From 1919 to Circa 1920 - "NewHolme", Westella Rd. Yelverton, Devon.
Circa 1921 to 1933 - 50, De Villiers Avenue, Great Crosby, Liverpool.

147

THETIS - The Admiralty Regrets –The Disaster in Liverpool Bay

by C. Warren & J. Benson

The definitive minute by minute account of this terrible tragedy in 1939 when 99 men lost their lives as HM Submarine *Thetis* undertook her first and only dive. With new photographs and documents as well as a new foreword by a survivors son Derek Arnold, and a new postscript by maritime historian David Roberts. Why didn't anyone cut open the submarine? Why was there no urgency in the Admiralty's rescue system? Did the Admiralty really regret?

ISBN 0 9521020 8 0   £9.50 + £1.50 p&p

HMS THETIS – Secrets and Scandal – aftermath of a disaster.

by David Roberts

The sinking of *Thetis* cost 99 men their lives and is still today the worst submarine disaster in British History. This new book contains interviews with relatives of victims; sons, daughters, brothers, sisters and those very rare ladies, living widows. Also here are never before seen documents from the time; Offers of outside help, Secret Navy reports and even descriptions of bodies for identification. Why did the Official Inquiry blame nobody, explaining it away as 'an unfortunate sequence of events'? Why did the civil action on behalf of the widow's fail? Did the Admiralty cover it up? How much did Churchill know?

How were those left behind treated? A huge publicly subscribed disaster fund was collected for the relatives. How was this managed and distributed? Who got what and why? What ever happened to the money that was left?

'a book that shocks…tells the hidden story of those left behind' - Sea Breezes.

ISBN 0 9521020 0 5   £8.99 + £1.50 p&p

LUSITANIA

by Colin Simpson - updated Merseyside Edition

THE definitive work on the real story surrounding this still mysterious ship.
On the 7th of May 1915 the Cunard vessel Lusitania was torpedoed by a German submarine off the Old Head of Kinsale on the south west coast of Ireland resulting in the loss of the vessel itself and 1,201 men, women and children. It also ultimately resulted in the United States entry to the First World War. More than eighty five years on the story of the *Lusitania* continues to be shrouded in mystery and suspicion. What was her real cargo? Why wasn't she protected? Why did she sink so quickly? Containing rare photographs from Germany and elsewhere; it is a truly intriguing and fascinating tale.

'*The Trusth at last* '- Washington Post
'*A book that clamours to be read*' - Observer
ISBN 0 95201020 6 4 £9.50 + £1.50 p&p

CAMMELL LAIRD - the golden years
by David Roberts.

Foreword by Frank Field MP
Looks back at the world famous shipyard's history with particular focus upon the 1960s and 70s when Lairds were engaged in the building of Polaris Nuclear submarines. A unique look at the history of this yard that contains many photographs and references.

'*Captures life in the prosperous years of the historic Birkenhead shipyard*'-
Liverpool Echo

'*Puts into perspective...the strikes...the Polaris contract...and those who worked at the yard*'- Sea Breezes

ISBN 09521020 2 1   £5.99 + £0.80 p&p

149

LIFE AT LAIRDS - Memories of working shipyard men

by David Roberts

When Cammell Lairds has gone and we are a generation or two down the line who will answer the questions 'What did they do there?' 'What was it like?' This book answers the questions. - Sea Breezes

A Piece of Social History – Liverpool Echo

Life at Lairds is a book of more than 120 pages about what life was like for the thousands of ordinary people that worked in the world famous Birkenhead shipyard. Contains many rare photographs of Lairds, its ships and its surroundings.

ISBN 0 9521020 1 3 £6.99 + £1.50 p&p

Faster Than the Wind - A History Guide to the Liverpool to Holyhead Telegraph.

by Frank Large

Take a journey along the one of most spectacular coastlines in Britain, the beautiful hills and countryside of North Wales and Wirral. On a clear day it is possible to see just how signals were sent along the coast to and from Liverpool. This book contains full details of the intriguing and little known sites of the substantial remains of the Liverpool to Holyhead Telegraph Stations. A second journey can then be taken into the fascinating workings of such a telegraph and those people involved in creating and using the signalling system and what life was really like living and working at the telegraph stations more than 100 years ago.

ISBN 09521020 9 9   £8.95 + £1.50 p&p

Iron Clipper – 'Tayleur' – the White Star Line's 'First Titanic'

by H.F. Starkey

'Iron Clipper' is subtitled 'The First Titanic' for it tells the story of the first White Star liner to be lost on her maiden voyage. Built on the Upper Mersey at Warrington, the *'Tayleur'* tragedy of 1854 and the *'Titanic'* catastrophe of 1912 are disasters which have so much in common that the many coincidences make this factual book appear to be a work which is stranger than fiction.

ISBN 1 902964 00 4   £7.50+ £1.40 p&p

Schooner Port - Two Centuries of Upper Mersey Sail

by H.F. Starkey

Schooner Port tells the story of the part Runcorn and navigation of the upper Mersey played in the Industrial Revolution and of the contribution of merchants, the shipbuilders, and the crews in making Britain 'The Workshop of the World'. Also recounted is something of the courage and tragedy, which was the lot of many flatmen and seamen who helped build British industry on the strength of the shipping fleet.

'Recognised as the only authoritative work on this particular subject '- Sea Breezes

'Packed with hard facts and illustrated with some rare old photographs, this rare book should command a wide readership'. - Liverpool Echo

ISBN 0 9521020 5 6   £8.95 + £1.50 p&p

In association with

B B C RADIO MERSEYSIDE

ALL at SEA
Memories of Maritime Merseyside
Compiled by Ev Draper
Foreword by Radio Merseyside's Linda McDermott
Introduction by David Roberts - Maritime Historian

A new book in conjunction with Radio Merseyside's programme of the same name brings the voices of Merseyside seafarers and their lives to the printed page. Here are the stories of brave men, now pensioners, who survived horrendous incidents in the last two wars; stories of luxury liners, from Captains to cabin crew, of young lads forging their identity cards to get away to sea, and of their first eye-opening voyages.

ALL at SEA brings back the sounds and the smells of the docks, which remain vivid in so many people's minds, of busy tugs up and down the river, of men lost at sea; of women serving their country in different ways, and of those who provided guiding lights home. But through all the stories, there's one shining thread, the pride of Merseysiders in their seagoing traditions.

It could be said that there will be many tales that have not been included, shipping lines that are not mentioned, vessels, people and places that are not within these pages. However what Ev Draper has been able to do in this slim volume that contains so much, is to give a flavour, a scent, and an image of life at sea and ashore. If you want historical accounts, with specific data, this is not the book for you.

But if you want stories of the sea, told from the heart, by real people about real times and places, then this is a book for you.

ISBN 1 902964 12 8   £5.99 Plus £1.25 p&p

THE GOLDEN WRECK - THE TRAGEDY OF THE *ROYAL CHARTER*
by Alexander Mckee

The effects great of the great hurricane of October 1859 were to shock the nation. 133 ships were sunk, 90 were badly damaged and almost 800 people lost their lives.

More than half of those that perished were on one ship - The *Royal Charter*.

The Royal Charter has a special place in maritime history as one of the greatest ever peacetime disasters. Her story too is one of incredible bad luck...had she come to grief just yards away from the unforgiving rocks that destroyed her she would have grounded upon a stony beach where it is likely that most of her passengers and crew would have been able to walk off.

She was also an extraordinary vessel in that she belonged to that crossover period between sail and steam when the steam engine was unproven and unreliable, not only that but coal was bulky and expensive whilst the wind, though erratic, was free of charge. She was a compromise, a sailing ship with an engine, not a main engine but a small 'auxiliary' engine that would be used when the wind eluded her, to power the vessel to try and 'find the wind'. Furthermore the Royal Charter moved away from the tried and tested design of the fast clippers that were constructed of wood... she was made of iron.

She was built at Sandycroft on the River Dee, the next-door neighbour to the river that was to become her home...the River Mersey. Soon after she was launched...sideways because of her great size for the day, she perhaps seemed ill starred in that whilst being towed down the river she grounded upon a sandbank off Flint, North Wales, and suffered serious damage to her main keel.

On her maiden voyage to Australia she had to turn back to Plymouth, England after discovering that she did not respond correctly to her steering and shipping too much water during a moderate gale... she was in Plymouth for 20 days. She eventually completed her maiden voyage to Melbourne in record time and her owners were able to boast about their new service 'England to Australia in under 60 days'.

Just a few short years later she was returning home and was hours away from disembarking her charges in Liverpool... until, when rounding Anglesey on the northern coast of Wales...disaster struck in the form of a Force 12 hurricane.

The people of the small village of Moelfre, Anglesey came to the aid of the vessel and those from the ship who tried to escape the lashing waves and the deadly rocks. News of the wreck soon spread and the *Royal Charter's* other cargo, gold, became the focus of people's attention. Was all of it ever recovered? If not where did it go? The *Royal Charter's* gold still has the power to attract the adventurous and this book also explores attempts at salvage and treasure hunting more than 140 years on.

ISBN 1 902964020 £9.50 & 1.50 p&p

JUST NUISANCE AB - His full story
by Terence Sisson

The amazing but true story of the only dog that was officially enlisted into British Royal Navy. A Great Dane whose name was Nuisance, his official rank and name was AB Just Nuisance. Famed for his preference for the company of navy ratings (he wasn't too keen on Officers) in and around the famous World War II naval base of Simonstown, South Africa, Nuisance helped many a sailor rejoin his ship after a night on the town.
Today his own statue overlooking the bay off the Cape of Good Hope commemorates AB Just Nuisance.
£7.50 & £1.20 p&p

A Welcome in the Hillsides?
- The Merseyside & North Wales Experience of Evacuation 1939-1945
by Jill Wallis
A brilliantly researched book that is both informative and moving, with the stories of the thousands of children who left the dangers of Merseyside for the safety of North Wales during World War II, and the people of North Wales who received them into their homes.
ISBN 1 9029640 13 6   £9.95 + £1.85 p&p

VIDEOS

Cammell Laird - Old Ships and Hardships - the story of a shipyard.

After an extensive search for moving footage of this world famous shipyard at work a video of the history of this shipyard has at last been compiled. How Cammell Laird served the nation through two World Wars, building world famous vessels like the *Rodney, Hood, Mauritania, Ark Royal, Windsor Castle* and many more, up to the tragic day in 1993 when Lairds was shut down.
The story of the yard is also told through the voices of the men who worked at Lairds; Welders, cranedrivers, electricians and plumbers, they tell of the hardships of building ships in all weathers and the lighter moments that came from some of the 'characters' of the yard.

£14.99 including post and packaging in UK.

'All in a Day's work.' Volumes I & II
– a look at working lives on the River Mersey.

Just when you might have thought that the River Mersey was dead and buried the biggest surprise of all comes along. There is life in the old dog yet! The River Mersey is alive and well. Liverpool, Birkenhead, Tranmere, Eastham and Runcorn are still places that enjoy marine traffic and employ people working on the river. There are interviews with River Pilots, shipbuilders, shiprepairers, tugmen and dredgermen that show that the age-old crafts and seamanship itself are still as strong as they ever were. There is also archive footage of working life on the river.
Features Rock Boats, Mersey Ferries, the Bunker boats & crews on the Mersey, the Vessel Tracking System for river traffic, new vessels on the river, lockmasters and much more.

£14.99 each including post and packaging in UK.
All videos are available in international formats for £17.99 + P&P £3.50.
Please state country/ format required.
To Order Books or Videos Direct Contact:-
Avid Publications, Garth Boulevard, Hr. Bebington, Wirral,Merseyside
UK. CH63 5LS. Tel / Fax 0151 645 2047
Look at the books and videos via the internet on
http://www.avidpublications.co.uk
E-mail info@AvidPublications.co.uk